CW00780300

RIPPED APART

a city in chaos

RIPPED APART
a city in chaos

Bob Parker's story

ANTARES
PUBLISHING

Antares Publishing
Published by Antares Publishing, a division of Antares Associates Ltd.
Registered offices: 37 Kemp Rd, Kerikeri, Northland, New Zealand.

www.rippedapart.co
www.facebook.com/RippedApart.co

First published by Antares Publishing 2012.
ISBN 978-0-473-21539-2

Copyright © 2012 Robert Parker and Anthony Farrington.
All rights reserved.

Cover design by David Bassett
Cover photograph of Bob Parker by Neil MacBeth
Cover photograph of Christchurch Cathedral by Jamie Ball

Photographs are licensed for use in this book to Antares Publishing.
Photographs supplied by Jamie Ball, Neil MacBeth, Jo Nicholls-Parker and David Wethey.
Seismic graphs courtesy of NZ GeoNet.
Street map courtesy of Kiwimaps.

Design David Bassett
Editor Di Keenan
Printer Choice Printing

No part of this publication may be reproduced, stored or introduced into a retrieval
system, or transmitted, in any form or by any means (electronic, mechanical,
photocopying, recording or otherwise), without the prior written permission of the
copyright owners and publisher of the book.

Opinions expressed by the author are not necessarily those of the publisher.

Seismic Graphs

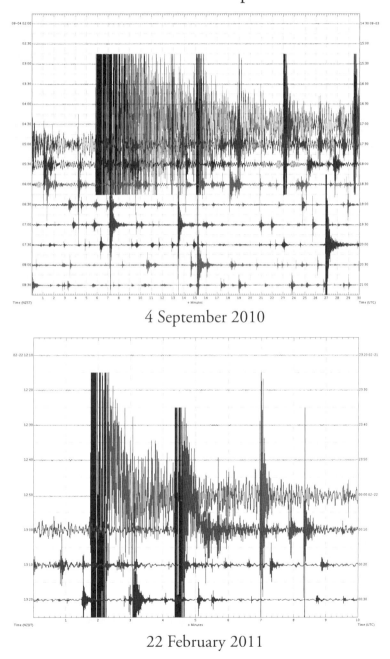

4 September 2010

22 February 2011

Graphs courtesy of the NZ GeoNet project and its sponsors EQC, GNS Science and Linz.

Dedication

This book is dedicated to the people of Christchurch and Canterbury who in the face of a great natural calamity have shown unfailing courage, strength, determination, and compassion. They are the inspirational heroes of this story.

Christchurch Inner City Map

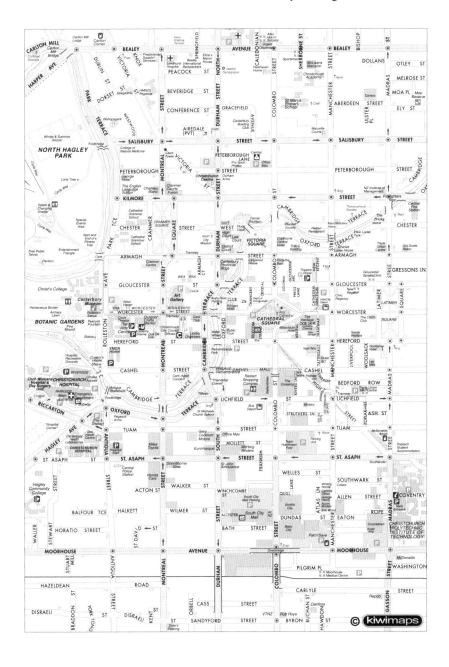

Acronyms

CanCERN	Canterbury Communities' Earthquake Recovery Network
CBD	Central Business District
CCDU	Central Christchurch Development Unit
CCHL	Christchurch City Holdings Limited
CD	Civil Defence
CDEM	Civil Defence Emergency Management
CERA	Canterbury Earthquake Recovery Authority
CERC	Canterbury Earthquake Recovery Commission
CPR	Cardiopulmonary resuscitation
CTV	Canterbury Television
DVI	Disaster Victim Identification
ECan	Environment Canterbury
EOC	Emergency Operations Centre
EQC	Earthquake Commission
GDP	Gross Domestic Product
GECC	Group Emergency Coordination Centre
GCSB	Government Communications Security Bureau
GNS	GNS Science (previously known as the Institute of Geological and Nuclear Sciences)
IRB	International Rugby Board
IRD	Inland Revenue Department
Km	Kilometre
LPG	Liquid Petroleum Gas
LOV	Light Operational Vehicle
LANSAR	Land Search and Rescue
OSOCC	On Site Operations Co-ordination Centre
PGC	Pyne Gould Corporation
UN	United Nations
USAR	Urban Search and Rescue

FOREWORD

Tēnā rā koutou,
E mihi ana, e owha ana ki a tātou i runga i ngā tini
āhuatanga o te wā.
Nōku te hōnore, nōku te maringanui
hei huataki i tēnei pukapuka.
Ahakoa ngā piki, ahakoa ngā heke, ahakoa hoki ngā
āhuatanga katoa i Ōtautahi nei
Ki te hoe ngātahi tātou i tēnei waka ki te ora,
ki te mahi ngātahi tātou, ka eke te iwi, ā, waiho i te
toipoto, kaua i te toiroa.
I te mutunga iho mō wai atu? Mō tātou, ā, mō
kā uri ā muri ake nei.

BOB PARKER IS a name synonymous with the Canterbury earthquakes and the Christchurch Mayoralty, but my association with Bob started well before then and, I expect, it will continue for many years to come.

I first met Bob in the early 2000s, when he was the Mayor of the Banks Peninsula District. I was relatively new in my role as Kai-whakahaere of Te Rūnanga o Ngāi Tahu and I appreciated Bob's strong leadership and support of some important cultural issues for Ngāi Tahu, especially around the reclamation of a former pā site. At that time I did not imagine that a decade on Bob was destined to play such a pivotal role as Cantabrians were to face the devastation of a series of modern day disasters, each building on each other.

In 2007, Bob was elected Mayor of the newly amalgamated Christchurch City Council. Throughout his mayoralty of the city we have gotten to know each other better. Our first big project together was the joint venture between the Council and Ngāi Tahu to build the new Christchurch Civic Buildings. It was named Te Hononga – joining together. It has immense symbolism. As I said at the building's blessing ceremony in 2010 "we have here Te Hononga – half owned by every citizen of this city and half owned by the members of Ngāi Tahu".

Bob had been Mayor of Christchurch just under three years before 4 September 2010 when the ground under the Canterbury Plains first shook so very violently. By then Bob had already established a leadership style that sought step-change for the region. His style was liked by many but there were some controversies, and not everyone was happy. Elections were looming and it was by no means certain that Bob would retain the Mayoralty.

Looking back, there is no doubt he was the man for the moment during our community's time of need. He used his amazing communications skills to good effect. Bob's familiar face and steady voice became our touchstone. As the September response effort kicked into gear we felt lucky – there was some significant damage here and there, but relatively few injuries and no loss of life.

In the post September elections Bob was returned to the mayoral office and life began to return to normal. There were a few tremors, and there were still some cordoned off areas, but largely we assumed the worst was behind us.

However, there was more to come, Boxing Day 2010, February 22nd and June 6th 2011 are all dates which are now etched indelibly into the Canterbury psyche. The loss of life in February was devastating and the damage unprecedented in our lifetime. As each of the large events unfolded, Bob put in a super-human effort giving media briefings to Cantabrians – the equally shocked nation, and the world – almost hourly.

There he was in his trademark orange jacket, standing in front of the cameras, calmly informing us what had happened, what we should be doing, assuring us that we would get through this – together. There can be no question that Bob was key to keeping up public morale during those dark, frightening times.

My enduring memories of Bob during these last few years is his commitment to the people of Canterbury and to the city of Christchurch. Like me, Bob is tremendously grateful for all of the external support we have received in Canterbury but he is only too well aware that the time will come for us all to reclaim our city and our region. He recently told me: "You know Mark, there will be a time in the near future when our city is rebuilt. CERA and the Government will have gone, but the people of Christchurch, the Council and Ngāi Tahu will always be here. And Christchurch will be a world-class city."

Mark Solomon
Kaiwhakahaere
Te Rūnanga o Ngāi Tahu

PREFACE

WRITING THIS BOOK has been both therapeutic and harrowing. Therapeutic in the sense of dealing with the stresses and trauma of the past couple of years. Handing some of it over to the written page has been like sharing with a friend. The personal load seems to have lightened.

The harrowing side has been delving back into newspapers, news clips and photographs. I realised both how much I had forgotten, and how much my wife Jo and I had been exposed to. Some scenes are best forgotten.

Again and again I was reminded of the scale of the event Christchurch, and Canterbury, has been through, and of how courageous and caring the people of this place have been.

From the chaos of the first hours after the quakes struck, especially the event on the 22 February 2011, to the inspirational grass roots response of our people, the bravery and dedication of the emergency services, the pain of dealing with the loss of loved ones and the enormous number of injuries sustained from the seismic violence unleashed on us, this has been, and continues to be, quite a journey.

It has been tough for my family. I have always felt that I should have done more for them during those first days after the February quake. So much was happening and so much had to be done that I could not find out for many hours whether or not they were safe. Fate was kind. Although they were all hard hit by the quakes, they survived without serious injury.

My parents (Audrey and Bob senior) live in Heathcote

Valley, almost above the epicentre of the killer quake. In this placid valley, the place in which I grew up, the most violent ground acceleration ever recorded in any urban area anywhere in the world took place. Aged in their 80's, they have been through such a frightening and difficult time. I cannot empty my mind of a vision of them being thrown around with incredible violence inside their house. Thinking of it disturbs me deeply.

Like all of our elders in this city, they deserved better from life than the hand Mother Nature dealt them that day. They live still waiting for news on whether their shattered home will be repaired or replaced, surrounded by cracks, windows boarded up, props holding up walls, the house rattling and wracked – yet never a complaint. Like so many others, it has taken a toll on their health. I hope they realise they are an inspiration to their whole extended family. I love them deeply for their unfettered support of me as I faced the most difficult professional and political challenges of my time in local government.

My sons, Nicholas, Anson and Dan have made me immensely proud. Nick, the eldest, had his hillside home wrecked in the quake. However, his three beautiful children, Hannah, Zachary and Madison, two of whom were at Redcliffs School the day the cliffs collapsed around them, have continued to prosper under his love and guidance. My youngest son, Dan, reported much of the early quake coverage for TV3 news. As he reported the city's anguish to a concerned nation we would meet occasionally in the broken streets. Every accidental meeting was a small bright oasis of family in a dark and often desperate time. My middle son, Anson, lives in Melbourne, and I was grateful he was out of danger.

Debra, my younger sister and her partner, Pat, had recently moved from the city to Kaiapoi, a smaller town north of Christchurch which was also badly hit by the quakes from September

2010 onwards. Fortunately, they were spared the depressing mud of liquefaction. On the day of the quake they located and took the family in and supported Mum and Dad and Nick and the grandkids. More big hearted and loving people than Debra, Pat and their family one could never find. That's the strength of family.

I also want to pay tribute to my wife Joanna, who stayed constantly by my side through such difficult and dangerous times. Jo, you've been brave and supported many people in their hours of need for which you have never sought nor received any real acknowledgement.

My office staff led by the world's greatest office executive Sarah Owen have been a brilliant support. I am proud of the Council, its staff and the work they have done. Also among the Councillors I must single out Barry Corbett, Ngaire Button, Sue Wells, Aaron Keown, young Jamie Gough and the wonderful Claudia Reid for constant support. It has been hard for you guys, but in my view you have stood up for what is right and fair, despite the slings and arrows of smaller minds.

I also want to gratefully acknowledge Tony and Esmae Farrington long time friends of mine. Tony encouraged me to collect my thoughts and memories, and worked to bring this book together. Additional help came from Dave Basset, Di Keenan and Andrew Tizzard, the distributor.

This book will never be, nor is it intended to be, a definitive account of what actually has taken place in the city. It is a personal view, a narrow slice of what happened, and being drawn largely from memory, there are no doubt a few inaccuracies unintentionally incorporated.

Although only a few of the thousands I have met and worked with in this time are mentioned by name, you are all here in spirit. The emergency responders, the international help, the volunteers, the fund raisers across the nation and the world, even the Facebook friends who unfailingly gave me their much appreciated support. Thanks to you all.

Kia kaha Christchurch. Never have I been more proud to be a son of this city.

PART ONE

CHAOS. THAT'S WHAT descended upon us that Saturday, 4 September, 2010. Interminable, wretched, desolate, chaos. Unbeknown to us, it sparked a chain of events so brutally cruel that the extent of the devastation we would endure was beyond imagination. Everyone agreed that Wellington, which is on a major fault line, could suffer catastrophes such as the earthquake which struck us; but not Christchurch.

The chaos stole into our city in the darkest hour before dawn. It rode with a cavalry of fear, frustration, pain and loss. It plundered our city, splitting our streets, felling our buildings, changing our lives. But, try as it would, it could not break our spirit – even though it took our livelihoods, our lifestyles and, tragically, ultimately, 185 of our loved ones. It robbed us of many things, including, to a degree, democracy.

It came on my watch as Mayor of one of the most beautiful and tranquil cities in the world: Christchurch, New Zealand's Garden City – a city which is home to nearly 400,000 people.

Its first volley struck in the middle of an election campaign in which some polls predicted I would lose the job I treasured and the opportunity to lead Cantabrians in transforming their city from a 19th century city, the centre of which had become badly run down, into a futuristic city that could meet the challenges of the 21st century.

The chaos occurred at a time when my opponent in the

mayoral race, Jim Anderton, was widely reported (rightly or wrongly) as predicting that the only thing that could save me from defeat would be an event of seismic proportions. How tragically prophetic! That still causes mirth; it is one of the more humorous things to emerge from our tribulation.

Chaos still haunts us to this day. It will for years to come. It is present in the streets, in houses, and in the empty lots where buildings once stood; where people once indulged in simple pleasures like meeting to enjoy companionship over coffee, or a beer, or buying meat or groceries. Unfortunately, for many of us, that chaos still resides in our heads.

It blinds us to the unique opportunities we must seize to build a legacy upon which future generations will gaze in awe. Through that legacy they will glimpse our resilience, our courage and our vision. Just as we see it in the stoic generations of Britain, Germany, Japan, Israel and San Francisco. They overcame chaos and drew from it inspiration: Inspiration to conquer catastrophe; inspiration to erect great cities; and the inspiration to build better lives and better futures. That is our opportunity.

As with most people in Christchurch, everything which was ordinary and routine in my life changed at 4:35am on that chilly September morning. Inexplicitly, both my wife Jo and I were awake. Jo, perhaps intuitively sensing something, had gone downstairs. I lay in bed contemplating our prospects and strategy for the days ahead. I suspected I was not doing well in the election campaign. I feared that my opponent's reading of the political climate might well be correct.

Until I won the mayoralty three years previously, Christchurch had been long served by a left wing powerbase. I was the first independent, non–political, mayor to lead the city for many years. Now, in its determination to win it back, the left had stood a formidable candidate – Jim Anderton. He had been prominent in local body and central government politics since 1965. He had served Labour governments in several senior positions, including Deputy Prime Minister. He was an experienced war horse. I found myself up against a massive left wing political machine that was determined to retake the city. If anyone knew how to run a winning campaign, Jim did.

However, I was not unduly fazed. I had endured some bruising encounters during my 20 years in local government politics. I had joined the Christchurch City Council in October, 2006, after making myself redundant on the Banks Peninsula District Council, having driven its amalgamation with Christchurch. After Gary Moore retired as Mayor of the Garden City, the people chose me to fill his shoes. The battle to disband the Peninsula District Council had been far more galling than the current campaign.

Some people heard the earthquake coming. Jo and I did not. We *felt* it. Every Kiwi has grown up with earthquakes. To some extent, we've learned to take them for granted – a few little bumps, rocks and jolts on which we perceive the ground is shifting. I guess, over the years, people may have become a little blasé. For decades it has been drilled into us that when we feel a quake we should dive under tables, or stand under door frames. This time, I just froze.

Downstairs, Jo lunged towards a large flat screen television and clung to it, not for safety, but because it had wobbled so precariously she feared it would tumble and smash.

We had both been through earthquakes before. We thought the brutal shaking would soon stop. But it did not. It grew terrifyingly violent. Never, had we experienced such violence. It became even more harrowing when electricity tripped, plunging the city into darkness. The noise was horrendous. The building, protesting about the vicious pummeling it endured, creaked and groaned as if it were shattering. Everything was crashing and smashing and banging, dancing to the tune of an express train rumbling beneath the ground.

I was in bed, yet I was being thrown about. For the first few seconds, I lay there expecting the shaking to stop. But, it did not. It grew more and more vigorous. It was as if I was in a washing machine. I was being rolled around the bed. I flailed about, grabbing sheets, blankets and the mattress, trying to regain stability. But I could not. Terrified, I thought I should get out of there. I stood up, only to immediately be knocked down.

It is pitch black. I am naked. I can't find my jeans. I don't want to run into the street naked. (We have subsequently heard that half of Christchurch sleeps naked and could have run out onto the streets nude that morning).

The room is moving in three directions. *I think I am going to die. Die up here alone. If I am going to die, I want to be with my wife, not alone.*

Jo gave up on the TV. Seeking better protection, she dived between a coffee table and a chair. Somehow, without her, the television remained upright.

She heard me flailing about; hopping, falling over and cursing as I tried to balance on one leg and get the other into my jeans. I could not manage it. Even when I tried to brace against a wall, I was thrown to the floor. "Get out! Get out, Jo!" I called from the bedroom.

"No! You come down here."

Jo could barely hear me amidst the din. She thought I was calling her to come upstairs. She considered she had a safe place and she was not going to leave for anyone.

"We've got to get out!" I called.

I managed to get downstairs and hunted for a mobile phone to use as a torch. Jo, seeing that I was dressed, suspected I would want to rush away. With the earthquake subsiding she ran upstairs and dressed.

It did not enter my mind that the earthquake's epicentre would be near Christchurch. I thought our tumult was due to Wellington being shaken by a massive quake. The capital city sits on the axis of the Alpine fault. My youngest son Dan lives there, along with a number of other people to whom I am close. Their safety was my immediate concern.

In fact, the rupture that caused the mayhem was only 40 km away from us to the west, near the rustic town of Darfield. Until it so abruptly disturbed the city's slumber, existence of the shallow fault line, just 10 km below green pastures on which animals graze, was unknown.

We did not realise it then, but we were being battered by a force seven earthquake. It actually reached 7.1 on the Richter scale. It lasted 45 seconds, which is an eternity in those circumstances. We thought it would never end. Nearly one minute of unrelenting, nasty, deafening, vulgar, violence. Its force was 35 times more powerful than the atomic bombs that destroyed Hiroshima and Nagasaki during the Second World War. Unimaginable!

It's shock waves rolled across the South Island to jolt awake people in Dunedin and Invercargill to the south, and New Plymouth, more than 500 km away, in the north.

I often wonder how old people in particular coped that morning. In their first waking moments, they must have thought they were being attacked; it was so violent. I have heard of one 89-year-old woman who lives alone and, to this day, sleeps fully clothed with a mattress on the floor below her bed. When an earthquake rattles the night, she rolls out of bed and drops onto the mattress. Then she wriggles under the bed and listens to the harrowing noises, praying she will survive. She has endured more than 11,000 earthquakes since that first one – aftershock upon aftershock; some violent, others barely noticeable. She is one of this city's unsung heroes. We have thousands of them.

The chaos that descended on our city has affected us all in many, varying, ways. My epiphany, while contemplating my doom, about how important Jo was in my life, led to us taking a vow that night: we pledged that never again would we be without each other; never be physically apart. For the next two years, except for one brief period after an earthquake on 13 June, 2011, we were seldom separated by more than a few metres.

Fearing aftershocks, we rushed outside. The violence foretold there would be considerable damage around the city; possibly even injury and death. Civil defence procedures needed to be instigated.

My phone rang. It was Michael Aitken, general manager of the Council's Community Services. Each of our general managers is delegated with the task of being a civil defence controller. Each has specific areas for which they are responsible should a disaster strike. Month about, each is appointed duty controller responsible for swinging into action should a disaster strike during their shift. Michael had drawn the short straw for September.

He said the situation was looking grim. We agreed to meet at the Civic Building.

But Jo and I could not escape. We were trapped. We live in an industrial district, in a warehouse we are converting into an apartment. A 2.5 metre high security fence surrounds our home. The only exit, through heavy gates, was blocked. The gates would not budge. They needed electricity to drive them. None was available due to the power blackout.

I searched in vain for a pinch bar. Jo returned to the house and emerged with a post that we used to jemmy open the gates.

Uncertain how safe our building was, we fled. We drove towards the Civic Building in Hereford Street, dodging bits of masonry that had tumbled onto the road. Fortunately, the damage did not appear too great. But there was no doubt the city had taken a severe battering. We heard its pain. It howled and screamed in a cacophony of car alarms, burglar alarms and fire sirens. It was harrowing.

Incredibly, while the city was in complete darkness, the new Civic Building glowed like a beacon. It is a smart building that produces its own electricity from an emergency generator fueled by methane gas. The jolt from the earthquake had triggered its power and turned every light on.

Information is the most valuable asset in a disaster. We had none. We did not know the whereabouts of the epicentre. I continued to suspect it was Wellington. We were ignorant about the extent of injury and damage and whether I needed to declare an emergency. I considered the quickest way to gain knowledge would be to climb to the top of the Civic Building to look down on the city.

Because we live in town, only a few minutes from my office, we were the first to arrive. We ran up the stairs, scrambling over plasterboard that had fallen from walls that had flexed under the force of the battering they had endured. Although the building is only six levels, each of those floors is similar to a double storey. As we ran up the stairs, the top floor felt a long, long way away. At least there was light and power here, unlike most of the city.

The Council had occupied the building for only a week, having shifted from its old site in Tuam Street. Today was scheduled as the day for the first public viewing of the new edifice. It would not be happening now; the offices were broken and uninhabitable.

As we rushed upstairs, we saw cracks in the plaster wall coverings. Lighting systems had torn out, and ceiling panels had collapsed. The higher we climbed, the more the destruction. Fortunately, we detected no signs of structural failure, mainly detritus from superficial damage.

On the top floor, cordons placed around my office to isolate it from the public viewing were strewn about. We ran onto a balcony adjoining my suite and gazed upon the city. It was hidden by darkness. I imagined the thousands of frightened people out there and hoped everyone had escaped injury, or worse. I doubted we would be so lucky.

Fire was one of my greatest worries. A stray spark could ignite ruptured gas and fuel pipes and cause a spate of fires throughout the city. I was relieved that as I scanned the void below, no glow from fires penetrated the darkness. The crescendo of sirens continued to reverberate across the city. Even from such a height, the darkness blanketing the town made it impossible to discern the magnitude of the disaster.

We went into my office. It was chaos. Items unpacked and placed on shelves only a few days earlier were strewn across the floor. I felt heartbroken for us as an organisation. We had been so proud of Council's new home. Everyone had expended a huge amount of time and energy to make the transfer from our old offices a success. It seemed so unfair that, in an instant, their efforts could be undermined so cruelly.

As we surveyed the mayhem, an aftershock rattled the building. Suddenly, we realised we were totally alone and vulnerable here on the top storey of this tall building. Frightened, we ran toward the stairs and down to the second floor which provides access to

Worcester Boulevard, where the Art Gallery is housed.

We heard a whirring noise coming from above. We looked up and saw huge fire curtains dropping from the ceiling. Because the second floor is a cavernous public area, the fire curtains are designed to isolate the space to protect people from smoke and flames. We feared we would be trapped without anyone knowing our whereabouts.

The curtains continued their descent.

The building's computer must have decided the last shake was too much. It began shutting down the building. As well as instructing the fire curtains to seal off the second floor, emergency lighting dimmed and power switched off.

We ran for the stair well, determined to get out before the fire curtains blocked our escape. (We later learned that we would have been able to escape, but we were ignorant about the exit route at the time).

Finally outside, we drove around the streets, viewing the carnage. Bricks and debris littered roads. Grand masonry buildings in the old part of town had collapsed. Roads were buckled and cracked. Police patrols were already busy, cordoning damaged buildings with emergency tape and searching for casualties. Considering the earthquake's force and duration, the damage appeared less than I had expected. However, it was obvious that some streets would be closed. I could not believe this had happened to Christchurch.

People who lived in apartments gathered in clusters, anxious and shocked, some still in their night attire. They mingled with others making their way home from the city's night clubs.

We drove around the city for about 15 minutes. The news media – National Radio and Newstalk ZB – began calling my cell phone. From them, I gleaned that the epicentre was in Canterbury, probably near Darfield, and that it was a force seven earthquake, which is huge.

Of course, I did not know the extent of the devastation, but from the media's information, my own experience during the quake, and from what we saw on the streets, I assumed significant damage had occurred over a wide area. My main concern was the possibility of aftershocks.

The media demanded answers, but I had very little to give them. I had been unable to see anything from the top of our building and my drive through the city had not been enlightening. They appeared to know more than me.

My intuitive first messages on radio were directed at our citizens. I urged them to remain safe; to maintain cool heads and not panic; to stay off the roads along which ambulances and emergency vehicles needed free access.

Often, in a catastrophe, people's instinctive reaction is to abandon their homes to seek companionship from friends or family.

My message was: "Stay off the roads and ensure neighbours' safety."

The plight of old people living alone and those with physical disabilities concerned me. Imagine being deaf, blind, or disabled and enduring those tumultuous seconds. It must have been absolutely terrifying.

My sister's partner, Pat, is a big man and a tetraplegic. I wondered how they had managed. Imagine: your house is strewn with stuff; you have to get your partner into a wheel chair; you have to get him outside. How would you cope? It still haunts me.

By the time we returned to the Civic Building, the first of our civil defence team had arrived, including Michael Aitken. He came in immediately despite his own home being damaged. A chimney had collapsed on his 90-year-old double brick house. He suspected other damage, but because his area was in complete darkness, he had not been able to assess its extent.

Michael had immediately driven to the old Council building at Tuam Street, which still housed civil defence headquarters. He reported that as he drove he noticed considerable damage, particularly to older brick houses along Papanui Road. At Bealey Avenue, a popular restaurant lay in ruins. It looked as if it had exploded.

Debris from so many buildings littered Colombo Street that he could not navigate it. He left his car and strode out towards the Tuam Street building. So much rubble littered the street, he quickly assessed damage made the building too dangerous to inhabit.

Murray Sinclair, our full-time civil defence manager, and Michael Aitken entered the Civic Building and tried to reactivate the generator to give us light. It would not start.

The earthquakes came at a bad time for the Council. Before leaving its old premises, Council decided to construct a new civil defence centre. We had only recently signed a heads of agreement for the project with St John's Ambulance. Right now, when we needed it most, we lacked a purpose-built base. The old building, which, in the interim still housed civil defence headquarters, was extensively damaged. Our new building had shut itself down. It was without power and provided only dim emergency lighting.

Ideally, we should work in a place with which we are familiar. It is important for the emergency team to have instant access to telephones, radios, whiteboards, pens, pads, pencils and other equipment essential for the job. Initially, we had nothing; not even desks. Because of the shift to the new building, we had not had time to even simulate a civil defence exercise in the new premises. Even worse, every piece of equipment we needed to do our jobs – telephones, radios, manuals, white boards, pens and papers – were stored at Tuam Street.

More staff arrived. Selflessly, they had come in to help others, to implement skills picked up in numerous training exercises, never daring to imagine that this day would actually come. Many had left damaged homes. Most of them had families. All had a choice: they did not have to stay. But they were there because they felt that this was where they should be. It was their duty. I was immensely proud of them.

They gathered in a large meeting room on the Civic Building's ground floor. By default, briefly, it became our operations' centre. Simple requirements started to trap us. People had another plan in their heads; they were nervous about making decisions in unfamiliar territory. One guy came in and said: "We haven't got any whiteboards."

I got angry and replied: "Use walls. They're white. This is an emergency! Get a felt tip pen and write on the walls; we can paint them later. Don't make it hard. Just do it. You're allowed to. Give yourself permission.

"I don't care if you write on the walls, just go and do what you've got to do."

They began writing on walls. The sight of them behaving like graffiti taggers inside the council's pride and joy provided brief respite to the tension and the sense of foreboding that permeated the room.

Within an hour of that first destructive shake, civil defence was in full swing in trying circumstances. Because there was not enough power available at the council building, we had to find somewhere else for our headquarters. We settled on the Christchurch Art Gallery, across the road. Although it has a glass facade, it is designed to survive catastrophic seismic events. This time they did not have to write on walls. Murray Sinclair delicately placed paper sheets on walls designed to be adorned with art; a blank canvas which would ultimately become a poster of the city's chaos.

Civil defence, for me, is an encounter with chaos. After an earthquake, much of the city may be convulsing from trauma and destruction. The streets may be filled with panic, fear, despair, anger and bewilderment. People may be injured, or dead. Houses and buildings may be destroyed; roads disrupted; essential services – power, water, gas, sewerage – disconnected. Risks of injury and illness may lurk in streets. Initially, nobody knows what to expect, or the extent of the problems posed by a catastrophe.

The challenge is to gradually reduce the chaos down and convert it into a management system. Only then can we deal with it.

As Mayor, I see my job as harnessing that chaos and kneading it into simple, manageable, components to feed to people to keep them informed about the true predicament they face and solutions available.

Success in taming chaos depends on the state of our information networks. At the beginning of a disaster, we must assume most of those networks are wiped out. And that is what had happened in the September earthquake. That is why I risked climbing to the top of the Civic Building: I needed to see the extent of damage and whether there were any fires. Fortunately, there were none. I hoped the view would provide essential information I could feed into civil defence.

I knew that for the first 30 minutes to an hour, the people the city relied upon for civil defence could be fighting to save their own lives, their families and their properties. Michael Aiken, unfortunately, had to leave his family and a house that he suspected was severely damaged. It did not deter him from playing the role expected of him. I had no doubt most of them would eventually report for duty.

Local government is almost a calling for some people. They regard it as community service in a structured way. Council managers, after establishing their own family's safety, will get to civil defence headquarters. It is an automatic response. I think it is incredible. They did not have to be there, but they turned up to help the rest of Christchurch.

Gradually, as more and more people arrived at the Civic Building, the spider's web of networks required to unravel the chaos formed.

Police and emergency services personnel arrived, logistics and IT people turned up – as did Council staff responsible for infrastructure and essential services. Their tasks were pre-ordained. They had rehearsed them many times. There is a structure to what they do. There is a manual that holds secrets evolved from mock disasters enacted over many years. Obviously, nothing in a disaster is totally predictable; therefore, much of their work is intuitive.

The Canterbury District Police Commander, Dave Cliff, was in Dunedin when the earthquake struck. He immediately drove back to Christchurch. While he was on the road, police all over Christchurch and from throughout the South Island intuitively mobilised to offer assistance.

Soon after the first violent shake, police were on the streets, cordoning off dangerous sites to ensure public safety and security. Others moved into suburbs to reassure residents that although power had blacked out, they would be alright. They also made sure there were no injuries.

When the enormity of the earthquake was known, many police were sent home to rest so that they could return to work night shift. Police were put on 12 hour days.

Information began to flow in. Initially, it was a trickle, mainly from radio. Telephones were useless because the thousands of people using them overloaded exchanges and cell networks. Even worse, cell towers were threatened with another problem – no electricity – which would deprive batteries of recharging. Cell sites would eventually crash. Talkback radio provided precious knowledge about people's predicaments in the suburbs and throughout the city. Scores of people breathlessly, nervously, recounted their harrowing stories: "I was asleep. I woke up and heard a terrible crash. It was the chimney coming through the roof in the lounge," said Joy of Linwood.

"I woke up to a noise that sounded like a truck driving too close to the house. And everything was shaking and moving. I knew it was an earthquake. The sound of things falling off shelves and crashing on the floor was horrible. I'll never forget it," said Clem from St Alban's.

"I think the water pipe has burst. We've got a waterspout in our driveway," Eileen of Addington reported.

Each piece of information was a tile in an information mosaic that formed a pattern of the extent of the city's damage

A picture evolved as police, ambulance, the fire brigade, the volunteer fire brigade, our own civil defence structures, which comprised communities in the suburbs, fed information into us whatever way they could – telephone, satellite telephones, and emergency services radios.

Civil defence personnel recorded each snippet of intelligence: addresses where buildings were down; where water mains had burst; where roads had subsided; where power was out; where sewage pipes had broken; where power was off and where there were a host of other emergencies.

Others scribbled phone numbers and addresses on the posters – scores of them: contacts for people who could provide assistance to tame a burst water main; to divert sewage spewing onto a lawn; to fasten a roof or door; to rescue a cat up a tree. The problems confronting us were boundless and unpredictable.

By about 8:30am, a comprehensive picture of the state of the city had emerged from a steady supply of data. We heard that muddy water flooding streets and properties in the eastern suburbs was widespread. People and cars had been totally immersed in it. We suspected water mains had blown. Later, we realised the problem was actually a new phenomenon to most people – liquefaction. It occurred mainly in the riverside and wetland areas.

Before becoming Mayor of Christchurch, I held the same position on the Banks Peninsula District Council. That role required me to attend civil defence briefings at which experts advised: "If there is an earthquake, there is going to be liquefaction at the Port."

"Liquefaction, what the hell is that?" I recall challenging the first time I heard it mentioned.

"All those fuel tanks at the Port are built on reclaimed land," they explained. "In a severe earthquake the land might liquefy."

"It's full of rocks and stuff; it won't liquefy," I reasoned. "Anyway, what is liquefy?"

Then they explained it to us. Quite simply, the force of the earthquake shook soils so violently that dirt compacted and allowed water to mix with it. It oozed out of the ground in a gooey torrent that uplifted and split pipes, collapsed streets and carpeted roads, paths, lawns and floors in mud. It even devoured cars when it caused roads to subside.

Now, we were told there was liquefaction occurring extensively in the city. Although I knew what it was, I understood very little about it. I had only seen it in the context of the oil storage at Lyttelton Port. I never imagined it would be so widespread in Christchurch.

Word came in about liquefaction occurring in many suburbs, mainly in the east in areas such as Pines Beach, Avonside, Avondale, Dallington, Burwood, Brooklands, Bexley and Spencerville. However, it was not limited to those areas. It also occurred along rivers in the north of the city in areas of Merivale, Fendalton, and in the southwest around Halswell. Inner city suburbs such as St Albans and Richmond were also impacted by liquefaction.

It was obvious that, while an alarming amount of damage had occurred to buildings throughout the city, liquefaction was going to be a significant issue in many places.

Gradually, graffiti on the posters on the walls, whiteboards and computer screens evolved into a mural of chaos.

The controllers, general managers from the Council's various divisions – roads, street works, water and sewage – led the team. They are familiar with each of the city's essential services. Their wisdom is vital to reduce risk to the public and to get the city functioning again as quickly as practicable. To manage the chaos, they apply a simple step-by-step logic.

Michael Aitken, Jane Parfitt, general manager of City Environment, Peter Mitchell, general manager of Regulation and Democracy Services, and Kevin Locke, general manager of Capital Programme, are the ones tasked with the responsibility for managing the city during a disaster.

They are powerful people. The Civil Defence Act empowers them to restrict people from going anywhere. They have authority to close off air spaces, they can requisition resources and they are empowered to direct police and fire services.

I watched the team systematically harnessing the chaos. They worked instinctively, diligently. Because the process had been well rehearsed in exercises, they could actually implement it in a darkened room, if required. To a degree, that is what the controllers were doing, because they did not get to view the carnage for themselves. Their eyes were those of people all over Christchurch who sent in reports.

Eventually, every aspect of the city's pain was contained in that mural of chaos.

Because the shaking had been so severe, we prepared ourselves for grim news. History also told us to expect the worst. A similar strength earthquake in San Francisco in 1989 had killed 63 people. Ten months before we experienced this earthquake, Haiti was felled by a magnitude seven shake. It took a grim toll. Over 300,000 people had died. Another 300,000 were injured. One million people were homeless.

Based on these catastrophes, we feared scores of people may have been killed and maimed. We were immensely relieved when all the reports filtering into us repeated the same joyous story – no one had been seriously hurt.

The earthquake's timing was undoubtedly the reason for so few casualties. When building facades collapsed in Colombo Street, Bealey Avenue and other places, nobody was around for them to kill. Most people were tucked up in their beds.

I had feared that even there they would not be safe and that falling chimneys, furniture and shattering glass could have caused injury. It transpired that only two people were hurt in this way, although several reported miraculous narrow escapes when chimneys crashed through ceilings, or bricks from walls landed only inches from the pillow on which they slept.

The only fatality was a man who had a heart attack. We assumed he died because of the stress the earthquake placed on his heart. However, this cannot be proved. Coincidentally, Christchurch Public Hospital noticed a dramatic increase in the number of patients requiring treatment for heart related complaints over the next few days as aftershocks continued their relentless assault.

We feared we had gas leaking when reports came in that an acrid stench of sulphur pervaded the city. Fortunately, it was not highly combustible LPG. It turned out to be vapours escaping from the miles and miles of sewer pipes that had ruptured.

The smashed sewer pipes threatened to become a significant problem. People would be unable to use their toilets because they could contaminate fresh water supplies which were also broken. We urged residents to refrain from even cleaning their teeth with fresh water, let alone drinking it or cooking with it, unless it was boiled first.

Boiling would be difficult. The earthquake had blacked out 75 per cent of the city's electricity.

We also urged them not to use their toilets. Instead, they should place waste in buckets or plastic bags, rather than holes in the ground, to protect the city's vast natural pristine aqua flows that lie under its soils.

Briefly, we felt isolated from the rest of the world. Christchurch International Airport closed to air traffic because of fears about cracks on the runway. Main trunk rail services ceased after lines buckled. Road and rail bridges had twisted and collapsed, and many roads were unusable because of sinkholes, broken bitumen, flooding and liquefaction.

Many schools, some of which could have provided emergency shelters for homeless people, were badly damaged. So too were our universities and libraries.

Thousands of homes, particularly in the eastern suburbs, had moved, buckled, cracked, split and filled with liquefaction.

A large part of our city's character is based upon its Englishness. This is depicted in the scores of buildings and churches our forefathers erected with blue-grey stone and mortar from a Halswell quarry. Many of these iconic landmarks were extensively damaged, including the Repertory Theatre on Kilmore Street, whose boards I had trod as an aspiring actor.

Christchurch Arts Centre, where I regularly enjoyed coffee, was moderately damaged. So was Heathcote's Valley Inn Tavern (built in 1877). I had lived next door to it as a child. Many of the city's stone churches were damaged. And on the Peninsula, where I cut my teeth in local government politics, many of the Port of Lyttelton's brick and timber buildings were shaken to the ground. The town's Time Ball Station, which was one of only five working time ball stations in the world, and had stood there since 1876, was also damaged.

Reports came in from throughout Canterbury that many magnificent homesteads built by the province's founding families had also suffered varying degrees of destruction.

The mural of chaos appearing on the whiteboards and posters around us portrayed the sad picture. Christchurch's character might have changed forever. I was determined to get the city and its people back to where it had been before the assault upon it only a few hours previously.

Strain permeating the operations room was not the only tension the team encountered. While the controllers gathered information about the extent of damage to the city, we met with the regional civil defence squad based in a bunker at Environment Canterbury (ECan). A power struggle developed over responsibilities for the disaster. The ECan team wanted to take control of parts of our operation. I was determined not to accede.

Bad blood between our organisations went back several months, to March, when Government took an unprecedented step in sacking ECan's elected councillors and replacing them with Commissioners. It took such drastic action at the urging of the region's mayors who claimed ECan had failed to adequately perform basic functions, particularly with regard to the province's water supplies.

Although it was speculated that I was leader of the mayoral group, this was not true. Some people within ECan remained resentful. Staff can be as political as politicians, in some cases. They try to undermine us whenever possible.

This became obvious with problems we experienced with bus routes. ECan gave routes which Christchurch City Council's Red Bus Company traditionally had to other transport operators. They proved to be inefficient to the extent that police forced some of their buses off the road because of concerns about their safety.

Bad blood still existed in September 2010.

ECan employees tried to muscle in on the city's civil defence operation. I did not want ECan controlling our resources. Regional civil defence staff was not conversant with our systems and structures. I considered they did not understand our situation or our needs.

The structure imposed upon us by the Civil Defence Act has the three councils, Christchurch City, Selwyn District and Waimakariri District reporting to the Group Emergency Coordination Centre (GECC), which in turn reports to the Ministry of Civil Defence.

We ran into problems with an individual in the ECan GECC team. In our haste to obtain urgent resources, we bypassed bureaucratic channels requiring us to direct requests through them. An arm wrestle developed. They demanded we should work through their regional office, even though it would make the system slow and cumbersome.

We considered this unnecessary. We felt justified, in the circumstances, to go directly to building inspectors, engineers, and other suppliers throughout the country to obtain services and equipment we urgently needed to improve the dire condition in which the city found itself.

We had an emergency, I explained. We wanted action, not bureaucracy. This attitude created a lot of tension with ECan.

Their trump card was to remind us that the Civil Defence Act empowered them to direct our controllers. In fact, it does not actually work that way. Relationships are established between all parties over years of working together. One expects a degree of latitude. I was surprised at how difficult they tried to make it for us. Obviously, the regional people felt slighted.

Our team made decisions based on the best of intentions. It was true that they did not always work through prescribed channels. Given the circumstances, I felt that was understandable.

We sensed the regional civil defence people saw the earthquake as their big moment, an event for which they had trained their whole lives. The bickering continued and they were annoyed we refused to play ball. Civil defence for the province was, at that stage, headquartered at ECan, while the city's team worked from the Art Gallery.

Because they represented the region, ECan felt they should exert total control over us, including all public statements, calling press conferences and making day-to-day decisions. We thought this misread the situation. We believed we obviously had a much more intimate relationship with the city. We were familiar with all aspects of the infrastructure which was damaged and the communities within the city.

Although the earthquake had regional elements to it, it was not a regional event. Each of the councils within the area were in the best position to know the facilities, the welfare centres, the roads, the water supply and the waste water systems within their areas.

I have enormous respect for the people with whom I work.

Routinely, throughout a year, I get involved in civil defence as part of my job, although I do not fully participate in exercises. The city's civil defence team comprised of people with whom I had grown up. I went to school with Murray Sinclair, the person in charge. We were Boy Scouts together. I have seen Muz work. I trust him completely. I was determined that he should not be usurped.

As Mayor, I am fortunate to have unique access to people and places.

While this status can be beneficial during an emergency, it does not provide authority over the civil defence team. The controller is the leader, although, being the people's representative, the buck stops with the Mayor when things go awry, or well.

Our civil defence team generally accepts suggestions. They also accept that being the people's representative, my job is to communicate situations to the public, to deal with politicians and to generally look after political aspects. They do not appear to want to undertake these tasks anyway, much preferring to get on with the nuts and bolts work that they are so good at.

One decision that was mine to make, after consulting with Michael Aitken, was whether to declare a local State of Emergency. It had never been done in Christchurch before.

Obviously, Christchurch's predicament was extremely serious. Although, miraculously, injuries were minimal, our infrastructure was seriously fractured.

The decision to declare a State of Emergency has serious consequences; it could not be taken lightly. On one hand, the declaration provides more power to protect life and property; on the other, it is a pretty big call and not one I wanted to make unnecessarily. I did not want to be accused of crying wolf.

I could not take the decision on the basis of what I felt; it had to be a rational decision based on information coming into the control room. I had to wait until I received a comprehensive picture of the extent of the damage.

Michael had to make a case to support the decision. He discussed it with managers from other affected councils. One of his main concerns was whether the city had sufficient resources to cope with the disaster, or whether it needed help from Government. The decision's impact on the public was also debated because the decision could empower bureaucrats at the expense of personal freedom.

On the other hand, declaring a local State of Emergency would re-enforce the seriousness of the predicament in which people found themselves and provide the comfort of knowing they did not face their dire circumstances alone. They were not forgotten.

One of the ironies of the disaster is that while I wrestled with making big calls for the city, the rest of the country had more information than we did, because they were privy to radio and television reports unavailable to us due to the power blackout. While people throughout New Zealand, and around the world, had seen television footage of the extent of the carnage, people in Canterbury remained ignorant for many days.

The picture of chaos developing on our walls portrayed the grim reality: many shops and offices were damaged and prone to looting; although we had avoided loss of life and injury, people's safety was jeopardized by damaged buildings and streets; people's health was also at risk because sewage was contaminating waterways; and many homes were without electricity, water or sewage disposal.

After deliberating with controllers from the other councils, we declared a State of Emergency jointly with the Selwyn and Waimakariri District Councils mid-morning, 4 September. The central city was placed under a curfew from 7pm to 7am. We lived under these conditions for two weeks.

Each day brought me closer to an election to determine whether I would experience the privilege of overseeing the city's recovery. However, I had a dilemma: I considered electioneering to advance my own self interests, when the city was so badly broken, was abhorrent.

For a couple of weeks, its politicians, shaken by events that had crippled the city, had worked together for the benefit of its people, rather than verbally ripping each other apart. I sensed the public had little desire for a return to our old ways. Some were optimistic that this spirit of cooperation could continue into the future and beyond the election. Alas, it proved an illusion.

In our circumstances, who, really, gave a damn about whether Council was transparent enough, whether we had consulted enough, whether we had spent too much, or whether my leadership was weak or strong? People's houses were splintered, roads were impassable, sewerage was cut off, and water had to be trucked in because pipes were so damaged it only trickled through taps in some suburbs. To me, with everything else on my plate, arguing politics was tantamount to obscenity. I cancelled my election campaign.

It was not the first time I had been confronted with such a dilemma. It happened on 9/11 2001, the first day of my campaign to become Mayor of the Banks Peninsula district. Terrorists flew jets into the Twin Towers in New York.

Those terrible events also made personal politicking inappropriate. Faced with a dilemma about whether to continue, I stopped at a church at Governors Bay, lit a couple of candles, and meditated. I concluded that the often petty, petulant and, occasionally, personal, abusive nature of local politics seemed so completely irrelevant with that time.

Cancelling the election campaign was a risky decision. Opinion polls prior to 4 September had indicated Jim Anderton would trounce me. They gave him a 20 per cent advantage, although my own research suggested a narrower gap from which I was confident I could win. However, there was little doubt that I lagged behind. But no matter how I looked at it, I could not bring myself to campaign for re-election. After witnessing so much hardship in the suburbs, and riding the emotional rollercoaster of continuing after shocks – we had more than 2000 in that first month – I had no stomach for politicking. It made the muckraking, mistruths and pettiness of the political battle seem completely irrelevant to the community's needs at that time. As it turned out, the people of Christchurch felt the same.

My decision provoked Jim Anderton to accuse me of demonstrating weakness, not leadership, and of avoiding publicly discussing issues. The media, too, were unhappy. Obviously, head-to-head debates and conflict is entertaining. It sells advertising. Given the circumstances, in some quarters there appeared to be a disturbing lack of sensitivity to people's personal predicaments. Despite the pressure my opponents exerted, I would not be swayed from my decision.

My faith in a lack of a public appetite for politics proved correct. In one of the biggest voter turnouts for many years, the residents of Christchurch re-elected me with a resounding majority, almost 17,000 votes. I found their support humbling.

Jim Anderton claimed that extensive television coverage I received during the earthquake State of Emergency won the election. Who knows? But what I do know is that an independent candidate, not aligned to any political party, which is what I am, is at a considerable disadvantage. We lack the funds, manpower, and the political machine available to our party aligned opponents.

This is often noticeable at public meetings, and debates, where crowds are heavily weighted in favour of the party hack. The loudest applause, the most vociferous interjections, and the most boorish behaviour, can curry a media headline.

Against a well organised opposition, it is difficult to reach your community; every time you say something the party machine will counter it with voices lined up to contradict you. I considered that under these circumstances, the television exposure I received balanced the ledger and leveled the playing field.

What did that TV coverage do for me personally? If I had been incompetent, it would not have helped me. The television lens can be very cruel, as well as very truthful. I do not believe that since becoming Mayor I have had a supportive press. The television exposure enabled me, for the first time, to talk directly to people. They could see me for the person that I am.

I believe it allowed people to understand a bit more about me as a man. It enabled me to talk directly to people without being filtered by the media. Because of the immediacy of the situations in which I was broadcast, there was no time for editing. People got me warts and all.

They began to think that maybe I was not the beast my opponents painted; that I was actually a competent, thinking person. They could see that I understood and related to their suffering and hardships. Before 4 September, they may have thought I was a flash Harry with a gorgeous wife, too big for my own shoes. For the first time, they saw me as a human being.

The public builds those of us in authority, or in the media, much higher than we deserve, and imagines we have advantages and attributes that do not exist. Most media performers and actors I have met are often more flawed and insecure than ordinary folk.

I know I am nothing special. I am fortunate to have a few talents that I have honed from things I have done over the years, but I am not walking around seeing myself as God. I am riddled with normality, like most of us. My journey has taken me, through alcoholism, to the bottom, when I went into Queen Mary Hospital in Hamner Springs 25 years ago, to a place where I have been fortunate enough to rub shoulders with the powerful and famous.

I can genuinely say I have had more fun with addicts and drunks than just about anyone else on the planet. I have sat and enjoyed the company of down-and-out people. I remember what I was like then, and I know the action I had to take to move on in my own life. That has been a very powerful process.

The last couple of years have been more stressful than I could have imagined. I have to admit that on the odd occasion my guard has dropped and I have had the odd drink. However, I have learnt enough about myself and the pervasiveness of the disease of alcoholism to know I cannot afford to go back to that place.

I realised very quickly that alcohol for me is not about social interaction. It is a drug that enables me to escape to the challenging place in which I once found myself. I am determined not to forget the lessons of my distant past.

I feel that through TV coverage around the earthquake, people began to identify that I was just like them; that there was something in me that was genuine and concerned. I was not appearing on TV because I wanted to be seen that way. Like all of those with whom I worked, I was simply doing my job. I was part of a great team.

Victory's sweet taste contained a taint of bile. Some good councillors were swept away and replaced by people with little experience. These included Jimmy Chen and Glenn Livingstone, whom I expected would combine forces with the Left's incumbents Yani Johanson and Chrissie Williams. Two other newcomers, Tim Carter and Jamie Gough came from the city's wealthiest families who had large property holdings in the city. The other new Councillor was Aaron Keown, a member of the City Vision political party. The party's founder, Jo Giles, died in the Canterbury Television (CTV) building during the 22 February earthquake.

They joined incumbents Helen Broughton, Sally Buck, Ngaire Button, Barry Corbett, Claudia Reid and Sue Wells.

Just four weeks after the biggest disaster in New Zealand's history, a new Council took its place in the chamber of the Civic Building. Councillors would face the most daunting challenges since the arrival of the first settlers. Looming ahead was a mountain of work so critical that the impact of their decisions would reverberate on citizens for generations. To succeed, they would require wisdom, sensitivity, tolerance, capacity to abandon their own self interest, and an ability to work as a team.

The task would be arduous for any council under normal conditions; in our circumstances, it would be Herculean. Over the months ahead, the rebuild and subsequent unanticipated earthquakes would test the mettle of everyone around the table.

When studying those attending the new Council's first meeting, the shift, in terms of experience, ability, and understanding, was obvious. From this diverse bunch I tried to stitch together a team that would enable us to seize the opportunity to reconstruct the city in the best interests of future generations.

Initially, I was pleased with the mix around the table. They represented a cross section of citizens, which is what a council is supposed to be. However, councillors have to work together, particularly in times of disaster. Leadership is not an individual attribute, it is about the Council.

The previous Council had, despite our differences, worked collectively. Even when we lost battles we displayed a united front. That is a tradition in local government, which is entrusted with working for the benefit of the community as a whole. I hoped that, despite its inexperience, this Council would continue that tradition.

Unfortunately, within a few days I was disillusioned and it became apparent that often petty party political agendas would triumph over collective responsibility.

The Christchurch International Airport Company suggested a few days after the election that I should travel to Kuala Lumpur to help clinch a deal with Air Asia which was interested in establishing Christchurch International Airport as its New Zealand base. The airline insisted on confidentiality until an agreement was signed.

I explained to councillors that I had to travel because of negotiations that were important for the city. Immediately, Glenn Livingstone, a newly elected councillor, criticised me in the media for leaving the city.

It alerted me that this Council would be difficult.

Early in 2011, the United Nations invited me to travel to Kathmandu to inform the Government about our earthquake codes and procedures. The UN was impressed that Christchurch had escaped serious injury and fatalities. New Zealand had previously helped Kathmandu develop an earthquake building code. It considered that providing a personal account of the earthquake would inspire Kathmandu to strengthen its code. If it did not, the UN feared an earthquake could see 750,000 casualties. In view of the potentially high casualties, I thought the city would expect me to respond to such a call for help on humanitarian grounds alone.

Again, the same people publicly criticised me. On both occasions, I believed I was simply doing my job. In the first instance, opening up a new air route based on low-cost travel was in the interests of the city. It had the potential to create new jobs and increase tourism to the South Island.

I was disappointed that opponents would make cheap political capital out of me doing my job, for no other reason than that their mayoral candidate, Jim Anderton, was not successful.

While the criticisms were obviously designed to damage me, they also harmed the Council as a whole. It was particularly virulent.

Christchurch is a 19th century city, built to reflect the dreams and aspirations of its time. Obviously, the world is a very different place today than when the city was designed. Even before the earthquake, the city was incompatible with modern needs; parts of it were decaying and needed rejuvenation. Retailing had moved out to suburban malls and light industrial and manufacturing industries had closed. Buildings had deteriorated and were occupied by low rent tenants, which discouraged landlords from enhancing buildings. Trade was falling and, because businesses struggled to make profits, they were abandoning the area. Streets were considered unsafe due to high profile attacks on people. It was a classic example of urban decay.

One of my goals, when I stood for the mayoralty in 2007, was to bring the city into the 21st century by encouraging redevelopment in its more depressed areas. It proved to be a controversial, frustrating and slow process. It is a cruel irony that earthquakes have now thrust a huge degree of haste into this task.

Shortly after I became Mayor, we bought five strategic properties from developer Dave Henderson, who faced financial difficulties and was eventually declared bankrupt, for $17 million.

Mr Henderson had gained notoriety through a three year battle with the Inland Revenue Department (IRD). The department alleged he owed almost $1,000,000 in taxes and penalties. The dispute ended with IRD withdrawing its charges. Mr Henderson wrote a book about his experiences *Be Very Afraid: One Man's Stand Against the IRD*. It was made into a film entitled *We're Here To Help*.

Our transaction with Henderson brought considerable opprobrium upon us. It was misconstrued as a clandestine deal to prop up a struggling developer. It was nothing of the sort.

Mr Henderson had an exciting vision for redeveloping the city south of Lichfield Street, a depressed, neglected part of town which many people avoided because of its drabness and dangers.

The initiative for Council to purchase Henderson's land initially came from the business community which urged us to buy it because it was so important strategically for the city's future development.

Christchurch city grew through small business owners buying tiny plots of land on which they established businesses. The number and size of those lots is a legacy of the past that has slowed urban renewal. Much larger plots are needed today to construct commercial and retail buildings that will be economically viable. This can only be achieved by amalgamating land titles so they are parceled together.

Now that we are embarking on rebuilding the city as a result of earthquakes, the headache these small land holdings present is apparent. Unless those titles can be brought together, it will be impossible to commence any comprehensive redevelopment.

It is significant that Government, under the Canterbury Earthquake Recovery Act, has given itself power to amalgamate titles under legislation introduced to enable the reconstruction of Christchurch. In the years ahead, the Government may need to use those powers if persuasion will not work.

Mr Henderson had diligently worked towards amalgamating land titles to create sizeable land holdings that were suitable for redevelopment. This achievement made his parcels of land particularly appealing.

He was also a successful redeveloper, having created good environments in areas like Sol Square and His Lordships Lane. Interestingly, because he had strengthened his buildings, they were some of the older ones which did not fall down in the earthquakes.

Business people who alerted us to Henderson's properties being available, warned us that on the open market the Henderson titles could be split up. If that occurred, any chance of incorporating the land into the city's rejuvenation would be lost. They urged us to buy them.

Because of commercial sensitivities and the speed at which his business unravelled, the transaction was not as transparent as it could have been.

Although controversial, the acquisition has since proved fortuitous. It has enabled us to start the rebuild of Christchurch with significant chunks of land already consolidated. For instance, Henderson's land at Sydenham will probably be used for housing, bringing people back into a previously dead area. The acquisition gave us big pieces of property in the southern part of the city. Some is already being used for construction of buildings to house an information technology hub on the corner of Manchester and Tuam Streets. It is the sort of new business we need to encourage in a rebuilt city.

I believe much of the criticism I have received has been generated, not solely by political opponents, but also by developers and speculators. Plans to rejuvenate the city, particularly by acquiring land and using it for residential, as opposed to commercial activities, even before the earthquakes, were not well received by some vested interests. I suspect there was some envy. Mr. Henderson was perceived as being rescued by Council at a time when global financial issues were resulting in a number of financial and property empires crumbling.

Behind the scenes, discussions have often been tense. Bullying, threats and intimidation have been tactics used against the Chief Executive, Tony Marryatt, and myself. They are at the core of problems and controversies that have raged around Mr Marryatt. They are part of a campaign launched by a well known Christchurch businessman to get rid of us.

The history of local government is built on pockets of influence. Traditionally, the property development community and the business community have enjoyed considerable sway.

Established practice was that if you had money, and you knew the direction in which the city was growing, you could buy land for speculation. Then you would obtain a zoning change and profit from transforming cheap greenfields land into a suburb. That is the way the city grew.

We changed that practice through the Greater Christchurch Urban Development Strategy, which I chaired before I became Mayor. The shift in policy was made for the benefit of ratepayers, but it had dire consequences on a few business people.

Prior to becoming Mayor, I had enjoyed widespread support from the business community. That eroded after my involvement with the zoning changes. Even today, I am still suffering fallout from those events.

Under the old regime, the city faced an unsustainable future because, for years, while allowing urban sprawl, Christchurch had kept rates falsely low by under-investing in infrastructure. The Council had reached a stage where, by the time I had joined it, it had to play catch up. Our future looked bleak. An enormous amount of ratepayer money would be required to maintain an aging infrastructure. Demand for new subdivisions only exacerbated the problem. Compounding the problem is a growing retired population, upon whom even a small rate rise will impose a considerable penalty.

The established practice with subdivisions is that a developer builds the infrastructure and, when the project is completed, he hands it to the Council, which is responsible for its upkeep.

Pegasus, a lovely development just 25 km north of Christchurch, is a classic example. The concept sounds great: A new town where a developer builds streets, lakes, a golf course, and lays out an attractive suburban area. It is located in a neighbouring Council district, Waimakariri. Its proximity to Christchurch is a significant advantage. It enables Pegasus' thousands of residents to live outside the city to which they flock for work.

Pegasus' impact on Christchurch is significant. Pegasus residents use the state highway – that is all right, the Government pays for that. When they get into Christchurch they travel on branch roads throughout the city. Commuters living outside the city bring up to 30,000 vehicles into Christchurch daily. That places extra pressure on our resources.

Christchurch ratepayers have to pay for infrastructure needed to accommodate people from Pegasus. It is expenditure our ratepayers can not recover.

Through the Greater Christchurch Urban Development Strategy, we decided that all councils in the area would work together on an economic plan that contained environment, economic, cultural and social arguments for where land would be developed.

It enabled us to influence where development would take place, thereby planning infrastructure needs in advance, rather than following the whims of developers.

Some speculators were angry. They had taken a risk, and were caught with land they could not develop because we had changed the rules. Several of them visited Tony Marryatt and me.

One person, who had expected to make millions from a sub-division, told us: "You bastards have changed the rules on me. You have cost me a lot of money. I want my subdivision to go ahead. There is no reason why it can't go ahead".

We pointed out the legitimate reasons why it could not proceed as he demanded.

"You've got to change it. I don't care how. Go away, I just want you to fix it," he insisted.

"We cannot do that," Mr Marryatt said. "We are in a partnership. We worked this out with a public consultation period, and I can't suddenly shift the line just because you've bought some land and you're not going to make as much money as you thought you would."

He was furious.

"I'm going to get you," he threatened. He demanded we rezone the land.

We told him that we could not rezone it because the Metropolitan Urban Limit had been fixed and it was currently before the Environment Court.

"If you want that land rezoned, you must go through an appeals process. You can't just come in here and think we will fix it for you because you are a good bloke," I said.

He took exception to that. He also took exception to Mr Marryatt.

"You're smirking," he said to Tony, "You're laughing."

He was not doing that. It is not the way he behaves.

Much of the public outcry concerning Council property purchases in other areas in my view, traces back to this encounter.

Our's is a democratically designed urban development strategy and we are not in a position to junk a decision to suit one person. It simply is not fair. It would be immoral.

I believe that this incident has been behind much of the negative feelings directed at the Council. It has gradually infected more and more people. I do accept that we have, at times, played into our enemies' hands through poor public relations and poor decisions.

Probably no council has ever had to work under the strains imposed upon this one. As if that first earthquake was not enough, aftershocks continued relentlessly; sometimes dozens in a night. They triggered adrenalin and fear in all of us. They sapped our energy by robbing us of sleep. Although water and sewerage were restored quickly, people's houses remained damaged, their nerves frayed and, for some, their futures uncertain.

The quakes attacked us in swarms. Sometimes they had a Doppler effect. We heard them coming one after another, after another, after another. It sounded like Mother Nature had deliberately sent her squadron to attack us. It was unbelievable. They sounded like Spitfires in the Battle of Britain. When they reached us they rattled and shook our houses with a guttural rumble.

At night, there were so many unexplained noises. Jo and I would lie awake, listening. Sometimes we heard an unexplained boom, like an explosion, but felt nothing. We knew that something had moved underground, but had not created a shock wave. Other times, it was like an artillery bombardment.

A friend, Lady Diana Isaac, who was in London during the Second World War's great air battle over that city, believes the earthquakes were worse than anything she had experienced there.

During the Battle of Britain, people heard the incoming aircraft and exploding bombs, but they rarely shook the earth to the extent we were abused. Here, everyone felt the underground explosions as faults crumbled and collided around Christchurch.

I was extremely proud of our people at the Council. Despite the harrowing conditions in which they lived, they served self-lessly. Within a few days they had restored water, waste water, made temporary repairs to roads and bridges, and even collected rubbish on time.

All that was possible because Mr Marryatt had structured his general management team to, in the event of a disaster, run and repair the city as efficiently as possible. The Council has eight general managers. Four were appointed as controllers with civil defence, while the others were charged with getting the city back on its feet as quickly as possible.

While half the team dealt with the raw issues in the suburbs such as lack of facilities, damage, and so on, the others oversaw work on getting services up and running again.

When I hear some of the criticisms propelled towards the organisation of which I am proudly a part, I think: how can people forget how hard we all worked and what we achieved? I suppose in many cases people just do not know.

Mayoress Jo Nicholls-Parker and Mayor Bob Parker attending a service
outside the Christchurch Cathedral after the 4 September 2010 earthquake.
A few months later another earthquake destroyed the city's icon.

Photo: David Wethey

The Civil Defence team being briefed. Many had damaged homes but
reported for duty.

Photo: David Wethey

Rescuers pulled victims and bodies from the rubble and took
them to makeshift first aid stations and morgues.

Injured were treated at hastily erected triage stations.

Photo: Neil Macbeth

Rescuers smashed their way into high rise buildings to free occupants after stairwells collapsed and trapped those inside.

Photo: Jo Nicholls-Parker

Latimer Square resembled a refugee camp when hundreds of USARs pitched their tents to help search for victims.

A woman being rescued from the PGC building. Rescuers toiled desperately, with miraculous results, to free victims trapped under tonnes of rubble.

A desperate effort was made to save people at the CTV building. One hundred and fifty five lives were lost there.

Nature's brutal force was evident in Manchester Street.

Photo: Neil Macbeth

A mural of chaos formed on whiteboards in the Art Gallery
as information about the earthquakes' carnage came into
Civil Defence headquarters.

Photo: Neil Macbeth

After the earthquake, tourists escaped from Christchurch
by trudging to the airport with whatever they could salvage.

Soldiers from Singapore in Christchurch on a training exercise helped
New Zealand troops man barricades around the city.

Photo: Jo Nicholls-Parker

HRH Prince William receiving a briefing about the earthquakes after arriving in Christchurch for the Memorial Service on 18 March 2011.

How's My Driving?
0800 NZARMY

CNS501

Photo: Jo Nicholls-Parker

A Light Operational Vehicle driving through piles of liquefaction. The Army made it available for Bob Parker to visit the suburbs. Without it, many roads would have been impassable.

The earthquake hurled rocks, similar to the one beside this house, from the ground like cannon balls. Unlike boulders, they were not round. They had sharp edges that cut through fences, trees and buildings.

Thousands of people lost homes and buildings in the earthquakes.

PART TWO

WITH A FLURRY, Sarah Owen, my Executive Manager, handed me a sheaf of papers to sign on the balcony outside my office on the top floor of the Civic Building. It was a lovely day. Below, work continued on repairing the $750 million damage caused by September's earthquake. Many people were enjoying a lunch break.

Since September, we had endured 5000 aftershocks. Despite this, we were optimistic that the September quake was our "once in a 50 year event"; the worst we would have.

The Minister for Earthquake Recovery, Gerry Brownlee, and I, had, a few days earlier, symbolically used jackhammers at street works to announce that the Council had moved from undertaking repairs to replacing pipeline. Our intention was to show the city it was making solid progress in recovering and moving forward.

12:51pm. It sounded like a freight train hurtling towards us. The building lurched up and sideways at the same time. Sarah and I tried to run. We were inert; anchored by the earthquake's force. Then it tossed us in the air. We levitated a metre above the concrete floor. Sarah, still suspended above the floor, appeared to be hurtling towards the balcony hand rail. She expected to be propelled over the side. Powerless, there was nothing we could do. Sarah resigned herself to dying. I was suspended in space, as if levitating on my back.

Suddenly, the building dropped. We crashed with it. I landed on a wooden table. I smashed three ribs.

"Get inside! Get inside! Get off the deck! Get into the centre of the building! The balcony could collapse!" I shouted.

Sarah had landed between the ranch slider doors. Lying there, she tried to grab hold of a chair. I could not move. I lay on the ground in pain.

We could not get away from the balcony. The earthquake was too violent. It felt like being in a car that was rolling over and over.

I feared the balcony, which is cantilevered to the side of the building, could collapse; it moved violently. It rocked so vigorously, neither of us could move. I tried to get up, only to be smashed into the table again. Eventually, I managed to brace myself against the building's side. The walls and floor moved and I was pummeled to the ground.

The motion subsided a little, but I could not stand up. Pain wracked my body.

"Are you all right? Is it your back?" Sarah asked as she came towards me.

"No, no, my back is all right." I did not realise it at the time, but it was adrenalin that made me feel no pain.

I got to my feet and went to the balcony. Smoke and dust billowed from the ground. It told me buildings had collapsed.

"Oh! My God! Look at my city!"

I could not believe what I saw. The dirge of sirens and alarms began.

"Oh! My God!" Sarah called as she crouched on all fours, picking up documents, "I've got a 2:30 meeting."

Huge plumes of dust continued to balloon from the city. We

heard people screaming.

"There are people down there. People are dead!" I shouted. "People are dead! Just look at the city. Look at the city! What am I going to do? Where do you start?"

"Are you guys all right?" Jo had arrived from her office a few doors from mine.

"He's hurt himself," Sarah announced.

I had crashed onto a sharp corner of the table, landing exactly on a spot where I had had a couple of discs removed from my back a few months earlier. Fortunately, my back felt okay. My pain was from my ribs. Because of my workload, it was several weeks later until I saw a doctor who confirmed I had broken three ribs.

We inspected the offices. They were in total disarray. Furniture had toppled and filing cabinets had fallen and scattered contents over the floor. Everything was littered about the room: papers, pictures, computers and books. I sifted through the mess beneath my desk, searching for my cell phone. It was essential for the task ahead. Aftershocks continued relentlessly.

I found my guitar on the floor, covered in files. I prized that instrument. It had been signed by participants at the *Band Together for Canterbury* concert that was held at Hagley Park on 23 October 2011. Jason Kerrison, front man for the top Kiwi band OpShop, and his business partner Paul Ellis organised the event. About 100,000 people had attended the free concert. It was meant to help overcome the horrors that began on 4 September and billed acts such as The Exponents, Dave Dobbyn and Bic Runga. I had a cameo role on my guitar with the rock 'n roll band The Bats.

At the time, I suggested the concert provided an opportunity for us to reflect on how the 4 September earthquake could have wreaked more havoc than it had. It was a time to reflect on all the things we had not lost. Little did I know six months later we would lose many of them too.

A couple of general managers appeared and, without saying anything, booted open a fire escape door which had jammed. They ran out and down the stairs. I gave the only helmet we had to Jo and the three of us – Jo, Sarah and I – rushed down the fire escape.

The consequences of this disastrous quake raced through my mind. Not only would people be dead and injured, and buildings down; several major events, such as the Ellerslie Flower Show and the Rugby World Cup, just to mention two, would be in jeopardy.

On the fifth floor landing I saw a mate of mine. He sat alone in a wheelchair. Our evacuation procedures require disabled employees to make their way to a stairwell landing where they wait for assigned staff to evacuate them. With the building shaking, it must have been a dreadful ordeal for them. They had to wait until most of their colleagues had gone.

"I'll wait and take you down," I suggested. I did not want to leave him alone.

"No, we've got people to do this," he insisted, "you've got to go."

Another huge shake rattled the building, knocking plaster off the walls.

More disabled workers waited on other landings. I tried reassuring them as best I could.

"You'll be fine. This is a safe building," I promised. "We are going to get you out. It will all be good."

We were among the last to leave. Outside, people were everywhere. Many were crying, afraid and bewildered. The cacophony of sirens and alarms prevailed. The road and pavements were broken. In some places they had sunk, in others they had buckled upwards. We had to get people away from the building in case it collapsed. We herded them through bubbling water and liquefaction towards the King Edwards car park, Montreal Street, in case another aftershock wrought further havoc.

People screamed and ran in terror as continuing aftershocks ravaged the city. They abandoned their offices and vehicles in droves. Throughout Christchurch 30,000 grim faced, stoic people trudged to their homes. Some were smeared with blood, others were caked in dust. Most of them plodded grimly for miles, for hours; men in business suits, women balancing in high heeled shoes unsuitable for walking distances through buckled, broken streets and wading through sludge and liquefaction. Many saw sights they would never wish to see again; they helped each other, pulling rubble off the dead and injured, picking up the bloodied and getting them to hospital anyway they could. Scores of others lay trapped under piles of concrete and crumpled buildings. Too many lay dead.

Those who tried to drive home, gridlocked. Most did not even bother with their vehicles. They abandoned them on the side of roads and in parking buildings, and walked.

Thousands of people fled Christchurch over the following days. They left by car, plane and on foot. There was a constant procession striding towards the airport. Many dragged suitcases behind them. It resembled refugees fleeing a war ravaged country.

Others grabbed a few possessions, jumped into their cars and drove away. They did not care about gridlock, or rutted and flooded streets. Their priority was to get their families to safety.

So many residents abandoned the city that a national census scheduled to be undertaken on 8 March 2011 was postponed. Statisticians feared it could have been skewed by the number of Cantabrians who had moved out of the region and resettled in other parts of the country. Much of the census was to have been conducted from the Statistics Department's offices. Their building was badly damaged. A census had been cancelled only twice before – in 1931, due to the Great Depression, and 1941, due to the Second World War.

Many drove south – to Ashburton, Oamaru, Timaru, Dunedin and Invercargill. They drove to anywhere where the earth did not shake, jolt and roll. Almost all accommodation throughout the South Island was booked out. People's generosity overwhelmed us. Relatives, friends and even strangers opened their doors and their hearts to the refugees.

Nobody knows how many have gone for good. We do know that many families have returned. However, there is no denying that we have also lost many people. I am optimistic they will eventually return, particularly if we replace what we have lost with a safe, secure and attractive environment.

I supported people's decisions to leave. Our situation was diabolical. If people could move to somewhere that provided their children with a good night's sleep, good schools, a place they felt safe, a place where they did not have to worry about the next quake coming, then, obviously, they should go there. Why would you criticize people for doing that?

The media may have expected me to urge people to stay, but I did not. At a human level, I completely understood their need to leave. The last thing anybody needed in the dreadful situation in which we found ourselves was me criticizing them for decisions they made in the best interests of their families.

They are our people. We care about what happens to them. We know most will come back. There is a quality, a lifestyle, and a sense of belonging here that is very powerful.

People walked up to 10km home that day. It was their only option. Thousands of people streamed into Hagley Park where, fortunately, marquees were being set up for the Ellerslie Flower

Show. The tents were emptied of their contents – shelves, tables, indoor plants and exhibits – and commandeered for emergency shelters and welfare centres. Hundreds flocked there, that night, including guests, many of them elderly, from most of the central city hotels that we evacuated.

We did not have enough bedding, or food, to cater for the throngs gathering there. Somebody suggested that, to keep the people in tents warm overnight, we should take blankets from the evacuated hotels. The weather had deteriorated and the forecast was for a chilly night.

"Well, let's break into a supermarket and take some food, as well," I suggested. "There are lots of supermarkets with food inside them in Moorhouse Avenue."

We had no water in the city, so I suggested they take as much from supermarkets as they could. Because frozen products would perish due to a lack of electricity, I urged them to raid freezers.

"Grab whatever you can to feed people. Grab biscuits, packets of food, anything you can get your hands on. Worry about sorting the bills out later," I instructed.

That is what we did. A civil defence contingent, accompanied by police, took utility vehicles to supermarkets at Moorhouse Avenue. As it turned out, we did not have to break into them. Managers of some supermarkets were already there guarding their premises against looters. They told us to help ourselves to whatever we wanted.

They made a list of what was taken, and provided food for community shelters at Hagley Park.

I tried several times to text Prime Minister John Key about our situation. Lines were overloaded. I could not get through. At 1:15pm I managed to get a message out: "V bad John. Think we have deaths. People trapped. Setting up CDEM in Art Gallery.

Epicentre Lyttelton. We are getting some shape into this but picture not good."

The Prime Minister's immediate response was: "We will come down. Just organising chopper."

Many of my colleagues at the Council could not go home. While everyone else fled the city, they had work to do. Our staff is encouraged to check on their families before commencing civil defence duties. If they are anxious and distracted by fears about the well-being of their loved ones, they cannot effectively contribute to the enormous amount of energy, concentration and skill required to help the rest of the community.

We learned the earthquake was a 6.3 magnitude aftershock, which was not as severe as the 4 September quake. It packed a much bigger punch, though. Its shallow epicentre was only five kilometres beneath the Heathcote Valley, which lies only five kilometres east of the city. What made it a killer quake was its shallowness and its vertical movement – its upward thrust.

My parent's house sat almost directly above the epicentre. As I feared, it was badly wrecked. I worried about them and my son, Nick, and his family.

I had been unable to contact anybody. I had heard that the giant cliffs around Sumner, including those behind Redcliffs School, where two of my grandchildren are pupils, had collapsed and that lives had been lost. Nick lives near there. My sister lives in Kaiapoi. I was concerned that although I had texted them, I had not heard from anybody. I could not raise them on the telephone and I could not leave work to go to them. I had to keep doing my job.

I was not alone with fears about my family. It was like that for a lot of people that day. We could not get hold of the people we loved. None of us wanted to believe the worst. Unfortunately, for too many, their worst fears proved to be true.

Events of 22 February reinforced just how important those links with family and friends really are. It brought home the fragility of life. It taught me that these events do not care who you are, or where you live; they just happen. The events are random, and whether you survive unscathed often comes down to luck.

Late in the day EOC said they had a team going to Heathcote Valley. I agreed they should look in on my parents. Fortunately, before they left, I received a text from my sister informing me that although their houses were badly damaged, they had all survived and were safe at her place.

Living with that uncertainty was dreadful. Every time I paused, I thought about them. I kept convincing myself they would be okay.

Twenty key members of the team needed to deal with a disaster of this proportion were out of town when the earthquake struck. They included Murray Sinclair; the Superintendent of Police, Dave Cliff; Fire Service's Chief Metropolitan Commander, Dan Coward; St John Ambulance's Operations Manager, Chris Haines; the Canterbury Medical Officer of Health, Alistair Humphrey; and the Canterbury Civil Defence Group Controller, Bob Lapton. They were in Wellington addressing a meeting about lessons learnt from the September earthquake. I would have been with them, but for an important Council meeting that required me to remain in Christchurch.

On hearing about the earthquake, they immediately went to Wellington Airport, from where they hoped to get back to Christchurch as soon as possible. Ironically, watching television, they learned about the extent of devastation much more quickly than us. They saw the pile of rubble which was all that was left of the smoldering Canterbury Television (CTV) building from which the region's local television programmes were broadcast.

The building also housed a doctor's surgery and a language school. One hundred and fifteen people perished in its rubble.

They saw the four storey Pyne Gould Corporation (PGC) building had collapsed, its floors stacked like pancakes on top of each other. Eighteen people died there.

They saw the 17-storey Forsyth Barr building still stood but could not see that its interior stair wells had collapsed, trapping people inside.

They witnessed daring escapes as trapped workers abseiled down the side of the building, while passersby dragged others from the rubble, and firemen on an extension ladder rescued a woman from the top floor.

They saw our iconic Cathedral felled by an aftershock, and watched as terrified onlookers ran from its dust cloud. Twice before, in earthquakes in 1888 and 1901, the Cathedral's steeple had toppled. This time, the damage was much worse.

They felt impotent as TV showed an array of collapsed buildings, all of which were familiar; and bloodied, traumatized, people running for their lives and trudging the streets, their faces grim, as they purposefully strode home.

Along with most of the city, at home Jo & I were without power. Later we relied on a generator to provide electricity but we did not have television, and the city telephone systems remained overloaded for some time; we knew little of the scenes they saw in Wellington. All we knew, initially, was hearsay, and information broadcast by radios.

Murray and some of his team eventually joined us after getting out of the Capital on a light aircraft at 5:30pm.

By early evening on 22 February the Prime Minister had announced that 65 people were dead. We believed up to 200 lay trapped. He described it as New Zealand's blackest day.

Inside the Art Gallery, about 50 of us, many traumatised from their experiences, and the continuing aftershocks, crammed into a small space without communications, chargers for cell phones, or even a photocopier. We knew little about the situation outside. The world's media demanded information.

Sarah insisted the team pull itself together and venture outside to search for answers.

"Let's cry later," she said. "The Mayor needs facts. The world's media is here and he's got nothing."

She noticed the newest recruit to the public affairs team. She was holding a little dog.

"Go and get me some facts," she demanded.

The girl strutted out with her dog and roamed the streets to Hagley Park. Thousands had fled there for the protection of the green's open space. She recorded what she saw and counted people huddled in groups. She noted there were gregarious Americans, staunch Germans, and British dousing their fear with black humour. She found somebody looking after diabetics and others reassuring the elderly. We gave these snippets to a grateful media.

What we did not tell them was that across the road from the Park, at the five star George Hotel, people found the contents of the bar scattered around. It was not long before an impromptu party swung into life to relieve the trauma of the aftershocks.

Someone wanted to know who people should call if they had missing relatives. No one knew. Jo and Sarah worked our limited communications until 3am to discover the number was 0800REDCROSS.

A TV cameraman bundled me into a truck to drive to Latimer Square for an interview on TV One's Six O'clock News. Every time we went over a bump, I gasped because of the intense pain from my broken ribs.

Latimer Square resembled a war zone. Helicopters hovered

overhead and dumped water from monsoon buckets over the burning, crumpled, CTV building. Police and rescuers wearing yellow and orange jackets and hard hats sifted through the ruins, searching for survivors. Corpses and injured and bloodied people surrounded us. Desperate families milled about hoping for news of loved ones. And all the time the earth shook and rumbled and rolled without pity.

I was about to go live on the News when Sarah tapped my shoulder.

"Excuse me, but your high viz vest is on inside out."

"Oh, shit. We'll just have to leave it. It'll be okay."

Immediately after the interview, TV 3 whisked me away to their studio. Their building was badly damaged. The ceiling had gaping cracks and holes in it. You could almost feel journalists' adrenalin as it pumped a torrent of tension that only occurs in newsrooms during catastrophic events. Throughout the interview, the building shook and rolled and grumbled like a ship going aground.

Interview over, I was relieved to climb aboard an army vehicle and head back to the relative safety of the Art Gallery.

We had reoccupied Christchurch Art Gallery. My office was a couch in the foyer. I shared it with Jo, Sarah and members of the civil defence communications team.

All sorts of people began turning up to help. An army squad swaggered in. An officer generously announced: "We want to support you, Bob. We're giving you a lieutenant who will be your aide-de-camp.

"Anything you need, we will supply. If you need a vehicle, we'll get one. If you need water, we'll get water."

"We've got some man-power issues," I said. "You guys would be perfect to help us out with that."

The civil defence controller and police had discussed the need to mount cordons to prevent people entering the central city. Many shops were damaged. Looters would have easy pickings from stores with smashed windows and doors and crumpled walls. Millions of dollars of equipment and goods were lying about within easy access of looters. Police were willing to man road blocks, but that was not efficient use of their time. They were needed for so many other tasks, particularly maintaining law and order. While family violence, car crashes, and disorder had reduced, none of it had stopped.

A huge number of police were required for dealing with the earthquake. Their tasks included identifying victims, marrying up people with relatives killed or injured, and liaising with hundreds of worried families who had members missing.

Police had a massive amount of work to do and the military's involvement manning cordons enabled them to undertake their core work.

A similar scenario had unfolded following the 4 September earthquake.

"What we need are people to man barricades. You guys, in my view, have the perfect people. We need people who can take an order," I had said in response to the Army's offer of manpower. "They need to understand they have to stay there, even if they're freezing to death. And they might freeze to death, because it's bloody cold."

The officers had immediately agreed. I informed Murray. I was astonished a bit later when he told me that someone in Wellington had pulled rank and vetoed the idea.

"You're kidding," I said.

"No. They don't want the military involved because they

think it sends the wrong signal, internationally."

'You've got to be kidding me," I repeated, incredulous. "These are our people. Normally all we see of them is their backsides as they walk up a gangplank or onto a plane to head off to some place on the other side of the planet. Here is an opportunity for them to do something for us at home. We need our young people to come and work for us. This is a moment in which they are required. They have all the attributes that we need."

"Wellington said no," I was reminded.

"Don't worry, I'll sort it out," I promised. "The PM is coming to visit in an hour."

When he arrived, John Key got out of the car and said: "How's it going, Bob?"

"It's a terrible event, Prime Minister, but our systems are swinging into action. I need your help.

"Would you have any objection –I'm sure you wouldn't have any objection – to us using the young Territorial soldiers to man a number of the barricades around the city. They've got vehicles to keep warm in over night. They've got communications of their own. I need people who can actually go and do that job because there are a lot of dangerous sites in there. There is a danger of looters. We need to start controlling all of this."

"No, I don't have a problem with that."

"Thank you, Prime Minister."

I informed the Army that the PM had agreed they should man the barricades. I asked: "Who's going to say no?"

It turned out to be a brilliant move, definitely the right thing to do. In a strange way, people found it uplifting seeing our young soldiers standing there, providing assistance.

Now, we were doing the same thing again. The army blocked off all the streets that led to the central city. More than 3,000 buildings stood within the cordon. It became known as the

Red Zone, the area that housed the worst damaged buildings; buildings that could topple and kill passers-by in an aftershock.

Many offered easy pickings for the unscrupulous. Jewelry shops, still packed with gems and treasures, were accessible through shattered windows, smashed doors or tumbled walls. Because shopkeepers fled immediately after the quake, tills contained millions of dollars of cash. Computers, goods and equipment lay unprotected.

Of more concern, was the danger the buildings posed to the public due to unpredictable aftershocks. We did not want people entering the Red Zone because, if anything untoward happened, we would have to send others in to save them.

It was not only New Zealand soldiers that manned the barricades. Singaporean troops were in Christchurch on an exercise. They eagerly agreed to help man cordons around the city. I felt for them. Even in summer, Christchurch is far from tropical. They must have been very cold out there at night.

The military were brilliant to me. They made six wheel Light Operational Vehicles (LOVs) available to take us around badly damaged areas. Those vehicles were a godsend. They easily traversed terrain that was ruptured, rutted, flooded and impassable for other vehicles. Streets were virtually impassable to normal vehicles.

It became a daily routine for a LOV to take Jo and me into the suburbs, from 11am to 2pm, between morning and afternoon press conferences and interviews. Often, we loaded equipment – water, food, blankets – on them for delivery to a community centre. Sometimes the driver would stop, hop out, hold a map on the bonnet and survey the surrounding area as if looking for enemy patrols. It was surreal. Much of Christchurch did, unfortunately, resemble a war zone.

One morning, the army officers announced that some Big

Brass from Wellington wanted to meet us. They would not disclose where the rendezvous would take place. Strangely, it became a very clandestine operation, although it probably was not intended to be. We got into a LOV with our aide-de-camp, and his appointed navigator. They took us for a tortuous ride over difficult terrain to Sydenham, a suburb that is within walking distance of our apartment.

We passed through barricades and drove into a zone the Army had cordoned off to prevent people entering or leaving. It was a beautiful day, but a little windy, which caused a dust haze to blanket the city.

In the distance, a military vehicle, a Land Cruiser, approached. A corps of high ranking officers alighted with the Minister of Defence, Wayne Mapp.

We clustered in a little space. They wanted to know how things were going, whether they could do any more, whether Government could do any more. It was a very interesting interrogation, in bizarre surroundings, about how things were progressing.

"We want you to know that we are on your side," they announced. "We are here to support Christchurch, and we are here to support you, Bob."

I thought it was amazing. They wanted to emphasise their degree of support for the city and to ensure I was aware that if I was not getting what I needed, I should tell them.

It was the strangest meeting in which I have ever participated. We were standing in the middle of the equivalent of a bombed out area, with military vehicles parked as if opposing each other. A couple of soldiers standing here, and a couple standing there. I thought I could be at Check Point Charlie, or Sarajevo. It was totally foreign to me; not a scene I had ever encountered before, or ever expected to participate in in my own city.

This was the city in which I grew up. Streets that I cycled as a boy. Now, it was surrounded by fences, military checkpoints, tumbled down, broken, buildings; and here I am in this little military scenario. It was almost demanded of me that I go to meet them. It was not something I ever imagined would occur in my city.

The earthquake became the Defence Force's largest operation on New Zealand soil. Not only did the military assist police with security, it provided logistics, transport, and equipment.

The Royal New Zealand Navy, which had its amphibious support vessel HMNZS Canterbury at Lyttelton Port, provided meals for stricken villagers there. They helped survey the harbour and ferry food and essential equipment into the port.

The Air Force flew refugees from Christchurch during an evacuation of tourists in the days after the earthquake. In all, more than 1400 military personnel, and over 100 Singaporean soldiers, helped out.

The military's presence undoubtedly re-enforced in all our minds, the seriousness of our situation. In an odd way, it also made us feel secure and optimistic that our ordeal would pass. I doubt that anyone worried about a loss of liberty.

The reality was that, through necessity, democracy had been suspended. The authority of the city's elected representatives had been usurped by a cartel of bureaucrats under the direction of Air Vice Marshal John Hamilton, the National Controller of Civil Defence. The Act under which he operated imbued him with sweeping powers that had never previously been entrusted to anyone in New Zealand.

"We are likely at Cabinet to declare National State of Emergency," Mr Key texted me on 23 February. "But important for Chch that they see everything that can be done is being done."

Although I agreed the action needed to be taken, I was concerned that it might distance me from the people whom I represented. While organisation structure charts placed the chief executive, Tony Marryatt, and me at the top, alongside John Hamilton, they also showed everything we did would have to go through him.

We had run into command problems with ECan after the September earthquake. I did not want to be embroiled in a similar conflict with Wellington bureaucrats.

Communications are vital in a disaster. When done well, they can lift spirits; handled badly, they can be demoralising, add to people's difficulties and generate anger. They also appeal to egos which can create jealousies, surprisingly, even when you are working in dire circumstances, when one would think pettiness should not exist.

This became evident during the local Civil Defence Emergency in September 2010. I was as surprised as anybody about public reaction to my television appearances and visits to devastated areas. At times I was mobbed. People, particularly children, wanted to touch my orange jacket, which had become as much an icon for the earthquake as the red cones that adorned our streets, and hard hats and orange vests. Literally thousands of people came up to me this way. Others told me they felt reassured by my television and radio broadcasts.

This was to continue in 2011. America's NBC Nightly News broadcast on 25 February said: "He's been called 'the earthquake Mayor'. A former TV host, Bob Parker has used his communication skills to rally his people the way Rudy Giuliani did in New York after 9/11… he's taken on a caring, tactile, comforting role; and, goodness knows, the people there need it."

In a similar vein, Robert Hardman wrote in the Mail: "He has been a reassuring, composed presence, a Kiwi version of Rudy Giuliani, New York's Mayor on 9/11…"

I am fortunate that life's journey has given me skills and attributes which enabled me to communicate with people during hours of their deepest despair. I have been humbled by the way they have accepted me. Even today, at airports and functions, strangers still hug me and thank me. They fail to appreciate that I need them as much as they need me, because, like them, I am still dealing with the traumas of those times, myself.

That is why I was deeply hurt, and annoyed by a report that a senior ECan civil defence person submitted to a management review panel after the September operation. The report's destination was ultimately Government. He criticised aspects of the city's management of the crisis, and criticised me in particular. He accused me of dominating media activity at the expense of Selwyn and Waimakariri District Councils. He also recommended that communications should be taken out of my hands and given to the controllers.

Media selection of spokespeople had nothing to do with me. Christchurch was the biggest of the three councils; naturally, most of the media interest focused there. I did not pursue the media, it came to me.

The committee to which the ECan draft was submitted rejected it and told its author to rewrite it. However, it demonstrated the petty jealousies, rivalries and nasty small mindedness that existed in some quarters behind the scenes.

During the recovery phase, following September's earthquake, communications had broken down badly through lack of proper management. We had all manner of conflicting statements being made by the various agencies involved in the recovery: the Earth Quake Commission (EQC), private insurance companies, the City Council and the Minister for Earthquake Recovery, Mr

Gerry Brownlee. Conflicting statements emanating from within these areas created chaos and anger in the public's mind.

With crisis management, it is important to have detailed understanding about local issues. One needs to be aware of the different sensibilities and various communities within the city. It is also vital to speak with a uniform and informed voice.

Communities want to feel they are in control of their own destinies. This is probably more pertinent in Christchurch than in many other places, because it is a very proud city that has always adopted an independent stance.

Because of the structures created by government, the recovery lacked leadership. I warned government it was headed for disaster if it did not improve its communication on issues such as insurance coverage, the zoning and colour codes for damaged properties, demolition procedures, housing, and its plans for recovery.

A looming crisis in public confidence was only averted by the dreadful events of 22 February. I wanted to avoid similar mistakes occurring during the National State of Emergency.

"This time please keep me in key comm role now and after emergency," I texted John Key. "As soon as I am out of core comm role it weakens the impression of my leadership role. This must be protected this time. V imp. Bob."

The Prime Minister replied: "Cabinet has made the decision. You will be kept in key communication role. That's critical. Back down this afternoon."

On 23 February, the catastrophe in Christchurch was assessed as so serious, the Minister of Civil Defence, John Carter, declared a State of National Emergency. Consequently, several government departments immediately became involved in a city about which they knew only a little. John Hamilton flew down to take command.

Armed with the texts from the Prime Minister, I attended Mr

Hamilton's first meeting.

I felt disquiet about the whole thing. I thought: "Here we go again, this is the same old thing. These bastards are about to take over from us."

And who should be sitting at the table with me? The author of the damning draft report about my role during the September Local Emergency.

During the meeting, when outlining responsibilities, John Hamilton promised that I would have a key role in the operation.

"I am not having a key role with this guy sitting at the table," I threatened. "This guy criticised my response last time and if he sits at the table, I leave."

I never saw him back there again.

Despite having an assurance from the Prime Minister about my communications role, the same battle started again. This time, it was with John Hamilton, himself. As National Controller of Civil Defence, and a retired Chief of the Royal New Zealand Air Force, I suspected he had a strong sense of rank. I felt that he saw it as his role to conduct the big picture communications.

There was little glamour about working with the media. My day began with a briefing from the team that had worked throughout the night. The first media interview each day was scheduled for 5:45am. Interviews continued with various media through to 8:30am. With 1200 media accredited to cover the disaster, overseas journalists demanded individual time as well. Press conferences at which all media attended occurred twice daily, the first at 10am and the second at about 3pm. Journalists needed more one-on-one interviews from 5pm to 9:30pm.

The real star at the press conferences was Jeremy Borland, a handsome young man who used sign language to translate our messages to the deaf. He developed a large following with almost 7000 fans visiting his Facebook site.

My secret objective was to present him with at least one difficult, or embarrassing, word a day. He handled them all with aplomb, although I believe he may not have been happy with: gastroenteritis. Demonstrating it erupting from both ends turned out to be embarrassingly descriptive.

How they transcribe the word "munted" is beyond me. It is a term born from gallows humour which became a cavalier way of relieving stress at the control centre. Everyone at the Art Gallery gave their all, probably more than ever before, as they worked around the clock to control the chaos of the city. To be truthful, we were all a little scared as aftershocks relentlessly rattled the building. We were also hurting from worry about the fates of families and friends from whom we had not heard. The very nature of our work meant that there was a veil of pain around us.

Humour was a panacea. It was from that humour that the word "munted" evolved. At early-morning conferences, when assessing reports about the state of buildings inspected, we would classify them as either: munted, megamunted, or completely f…ed. Clearly, the latter was totally destroyed.

I deliberately dropped the word "munted" into a press conference. It sent journalists scurrying for their dictionaries. I read somewhere that it was a mediaeval term (who knows? Perhaps it is). The word went viral and is now local colloquialism.

In between media work, there were briefings to keep informed about the developing situation, ongoing Council business to deal with, and visiting dignitaries to welcome. Fortunately, I was able to push aside most routine office work while we focused on the disaster.

Tony Marryatt could not, though. He set about ensuring staff were informed about developments. They all had vital roles to play in keeping the city open and repairing vital infrastructure as quickly as possible.

A major problem was damage that closed the Civic Building. Staff had nowhere to work. Mr Marryatt's team set about taking over libraries and other facilities which became temporary offices.

Communications had to be established to inform staff about developments and priorities for getting essential services up and running.

I was adamant that each day, after the morning press conference, I would visit the suburbs to hear how people coped. I also insisted on seeing rescue workers who had a dreadful, demanding and dangerous job. I was determined to keep spirits high.

The public did not see what took place before press conferences. Conflicts developed between Wellington bureaucrats and me over who would make which announcements. The whole situation reached a crisis when they tried to sideline me and handed me trivia to deliver to the media. The bureaucrats obviously wanted to promote their man. This was how it worked in central government. They lacked sensitivity to the situation we faced in Christchurch. It was our community which had been brought to its knees. People did not want to hear Wellington bureaucrats; they needed a familiar face and voice with which they could identify.

The final straw, for me, was when, five minutes before a press conference, John Hamilton criticised me to one of my staff. He said I was talking too long and briefings were not finishing on time. He proposed reducing my role to that of an MC. This occurred five minutes before a press conference.

I mulled it over, and decided I had had enough. I left the press conference. Sarah excused me by saying I had to take an urgent call. She talked me into returning to the media briefing.

The Mayor of Auckland, Len Brown, had generously seconded his media manager, Glyn Jones, to work with me during the Emergency.

Glyn is excellent at his job. He is an experienced journalist, television producer and media strategist. I quickly learned to respect his opinion.

He immediately assessed the situation: Wellington was trying to muscle in on communications, and they were concerned they were unable to control me.

What they failed to understand was that the people of Christchurch had elected me to be their representative. Wellington bureaucrats would eventually return to the capital. We would not. We would stay here and endure together, whatever lay ahead. They could not expect to win people's confidence in one or two press conferences. We Cantabrians were all in this together for the long haul; they were only visiting.

Glyn understood this. We threatened to hold parallel press conferences. He questioned the Wellington bureaucrats about how many journalists they expected to attend their media briefings if ours ran simultaneously. He also convinced me to stay and hold my ground.

Many of New Zealand's leading business people, civil servants, diplomats and politicians were in Christchurch on 22 February, attending the US NZ Partnership Forum. The Forum is a high powered business group that is working towards achieving closer relationships between our two countries.

It comprised the largest US Congressional delegation ever to visit New Zealand, and included the former American Secretary of State, Richard Armitage, six high ranking US government officials, top executives from a dozen major American corporations, and the US Ambassador to New Zealand, David Huebner. While some had already left Christchurch when the quake struck, others were enjoying lunch with their New Zealand hosts. Most of the delegates returned to AMI Stadium. They were evacuated by the

US and New Zealand Air Forces. The stadium was wrecked so badly it has to be demolished.

US Ambassador Chris Hill, who had recently returned from working in Iraq, told CNN the earthquake was more frightening than anything he had experienced in Baghdad.

Some weeks after the quake I was told that US Air Force officers stationed at Christchurch International Airport for the American Antarctic Research Program were ordered to immediately evacuate the high level delegation. The orders had come from the top levels of the US Government. Despite the airport being closed to commercial aircraft, the US Air Force followed instructions and made the evacuation. A giant C17 transport plane was the first aircraft to fly out of Christchurch.

Subsequently, I met one of the pilots of that C17. He told me he and his military buddies had felt conflicted about having to abandon Christchurch. Their instincts were to provide us with assistance. However, orders were orders.

A medical conference, attended by 450 Australian doctors, was also being held in Christchurch when the earthquake struck. Some of those doctors were involved in courageous rescues amongst the rubble and teetering buildings. They ignored their own safety to perform operations and amputations, and relieve victims' pain until rescuers could free them.

After the quake, many of those business people and Australians joined the sea of humanity that trudged out of the city. Some returned to their hotels, only to find they were too damaged and dangerous to enter. Others walked 12km to the airport from where they were evacuated to other New Zealand cities. Fortunately, none was seriously injured, although many were shaken.

Because they could not enter their hotels, they left Christchurch without any possessions or passports.

Over time, we retrieved their belongings before the hotels

were demolished. We returned each bag to its owner and inserted a letter to them which said:

> *Today your luggage has been returned to you after being removed from the Christchurch City Central Business District. The removal of the luggage from the CBD has been a painstaking process and is a first step for our tourism industry to rebuild itself after the two large earthquakes that have shaken the city.*
>
> *I am sorry to learn that your stay in our lovely city was interrupted by the earthquake on February 22. I hope that you were able to continue with your journey without too many difficulties.*
>
> *We are now focusing on the rebuilding of the city and I hope that you will visit our lovely city again in the near future.*
>
> *My very best wishes to you.*
> *Kind regards*
> *Bob Parker.*
> *MAYOR*

Many responded with gratitude and promised to return in the future. Typical was a letter from Sam Feola, Program Director, Raytheon Polar Services:

> *On behalf of the U. S. Antarctic Program, I would like to thank your office and CERA for your inexhaustible efforts to retrieve luggage from Christchurch hotels.*
>
> *For more than 50 years, US Antarctic Program participants have enjoyed the beauty and hospitality of your city as we travel to and from Antarctica. When the February 22 earthquake struck we had nearly 600 personnel in the Christchurch area, most having just spent six months or longer and Antarctica.*

Hundreds of our people had their luggage trapped inside their hotel rooms. These items not only included the normal tourist bags of clothing and passports, but also cameras with six months of Antarctic memories and laptop computers with business documents.

Due to the brave efforts of your citizens who have risked their lives to retrieve bags out of the frail buildings, we have extremely grateful employees. A typical response upon learning their bags are being shipped to them is this, "That's great news! I have missed my items very much. I would like to thank the recovery teams for their bravery and thank everyone else for their continued efforts to revive the beautiful city of Christchurch."

And so, on behalf of all of us who are privileged to know Christchurch, we thank you for your continued efforts.

Sincerely,

Sam Feola.

Despite the glass wrapped around its 14 metre high façade like curling waves, we were confident the Art Gallery was safe. A few years previously, engineers had scoured the city to identify the safest buildings from which we could operate in circumstances similar to those we now faced. Two buildings met the criteria: the Convention Centre and the Art Gallery.

Because the engineers expressed some reservations about the Convention Centre's walls, we settled on the Gallery as an alternative to the Civic Building. It proved a wise decision. The earthquake extensively damaged the Convention Centre. It has been demolished.

Incredibly, only one pane in the Gallery's glass facade cracked during all those earthquakes. Designed by Australians, and frail in appearance, the Art Gallery has ridden everything the earthquakes have thrown at it. The only damage has been inside, where a couple of panels fell from the ceiling and a heavy cash donation box toppled.

Fortunately, only 22 works of art in the $150 million collection were damaged. While some works fell from walls and plinths, damage was largely confined to a few chipped ceramic items and gilt frames. The Gallery's insurance claim was only $22,000. Many households' claims were far higher than that.

However, the Art Gallery did not escape totally unscathed. At the time we were unaware of the extent of the damage inflicted upon it. The platform on which it is built has subsided. This needs to be remedied before the building reopens.

Gallery staff devised a unique method of assessing the magnitude of aftershocks. They would rush in to scrutinise a John Reynolds work *Table of Dynasties* which comprised 1652 painted canvases stacked on top of each other. They believed that the number of paintings that had moved indicated whether a shake was a force three, four or five etc.

Needless to say, Gallery staff was not enamoured about our invasion. John Hamilton and Gerry Brownlee requisitioned the office of the Gallery Director, Jenny Harper. Other space was taken over for the Prime Minister and visiting dignitaries who included the Governor General, Cabinet Ministers, and celebrities brought in to give Christchurch thumbs up. They included Prince William, actor Russell Crowe, movie producer James Cameron, model Rachel Hunter and All Black captain Richie McCaw.

Eventually, as the National Crisis Management Centre set up, all the offices were taken over. The civil defence contingent grew from 50, that first day, to 500. About 1200 media clamoured about.

To ensure John Hamilton never forgot the identity of the rightful occupier of the space, Jenny made a daily pilgrimage to the office to enquire how much longer he might be there.

Staff watched, horrified, as the civil defence team stormed the hallowed halls. Normality and decorum were replaced with a battalion of people in fluorescent vests and hard hats, and scruffy journalists with an assortment of microphones and cameras. Customary whispers of appreciation for the masterpieces on display were replaced by a hubbub of tension, black humour, and disdain for the treasures surrounding them.

Immediately they entered the building, the civil defence team swooped on the Gallery's computers, desks, telephones, office chairs, photocopiers, fax machines and other equipment. They claimed them as their own. The vanquished Gallery staff was gradually pushed out of their offices into corners at the back of the building.

The staff, instilled with the finesse necessary to care for some of New Zealand's most delicate treasures, could be excused for thinking they had been invaded by philistines. The invaders brought many irritants: for instance, staff had to be careful where they trod. Soldiers, after spending nights manning barricades, slept in corridors. Toilet floors were soggy. Clothes were left hanging in cubicles. Crumbs, crusts and bits of food surrounded desks where stressed civil defence people snatched meals while trying to unravel chaos in the city.

The paintings required careful humidity control. With crowds teeming in and out of the building, as if it were Wellington Railway Station at peak hours, humidity fluctuated markedly.

Staff reverently removed paintings 36 hours after the invasion began. They insisted that only they, not the philistines, should handle the delicate works.

An Army officer rang the Deputy Director, Blair Jackson, at midnight to say he wanted to remove a Van der Velden exhibit because emergency workers needed the space. He refused permission, but promised to have staff dismantle it at 7am.

The Army had not previously shown finesse when handling art. It had damaged a large Andrew Drummond sculpture in the foyer that it tried to remove with a fork lift.

The security of artwork may have been compromised when loading bays were seized by a logistics team. Doors were left open to provide access for a huge amount of equipment to move through them – vests, hardhats, blankets, first aid kits, water bottles, steel capped boots, food, copy paper and torches…

Then they had to get garbage out. Rubbish removal increased threefold. So did vermin control. River rats, sparrows, ants and silverfish invaded the Gallery. All posed threats to the treasures. On one occasion, Jenny was seen chasing a sparrow with a butterfly net.

Because sewage disposal systems were unavailable throughout the city, and we had hundreds of people in the Art Gallery, we installed dozens of portaloos and a large toilet system designed to cater for big events. It was emblazoned with a sign "Royal Flush".

I will never forget the bizarre juxtaposition of those first days when we worked surrounded by great works of art, while outside the city was filled with chaos and carnage. It was surreal. Although it is New Zealand's second largest city, Christchurch is really a small close-knit community. Many of the emergency workers knew people lost in the buildings. Several others had lost their homes, or were injured themselves. They still turned up to help.

Murray Sinclair toiled aware that, not far away, a cousin could be dead. Doggedly, he worked on. As with everyone involved in the emergency, he turned his emotions into energy; the technique enabled them to continue the task expected of them. His cousin's death was confirmed two days later. Only a small fragment of his body was found.

"You have to block it out. You know everybody is doing their best. People were out there searching for him. Firefighters, police, St John's; each does what they have to do to the best of their ability. There is nothing anyone else could do to help my cousin," he said.

There was not much time for dwelling on tragedies, anyway. Most of us had to feed questions from staff or media, solve problems, consider dilemmas, and make quick decisions. Running on adrenalin, we were all wired to the task.

Often, the building would tremble and rattle as another quake rumbled through Christchurch. En masse, we would catch our breath and wait expectantly, anticipating what might come. The ensuing silence made a powerful statement. None of us was immune to fear.

"That was a 4.4!" Somebody would shout, relieving the tension.

"No. It was only a 3.7!" Another person would counter.

"Bull shit! It was a five."

"Naw! It was only a soldier having a dump," a voice suggested.

Black humour buried fear.

Relieved, everyone returned to the tasks at hand.

No matter how hard we worked, the reality of our task was always present – just a few blocks away people were entombed in tumbled buildings. Many were dead. We suspected some of those buried under tonnes of concrete could still be alive, but nobody knew where they were, or how we could get to them. As desperate as we were to rescue them all, we knew that we would not. And time was running out.

Our resolve intensified with knowledge that it was not strangers entangled in the rubble. Christchurch is a village. We all knew people who were trapped, or dead. They lay in the buildings, the streets, the tracks and the places we all used. It could have been any of us who, like them, was unfortunate to be there at the wrong time. We had all ridden a bus down Colombo Street, just like bus number 702 which was still there with eight bodies inside; citizens who perished when masonry fell from above. None of those were safe locations at 12:51pm on 22 February 2011.

Some of our team had been in those same places on their lunch break when the earthquake ripped the city apart. Some narrowly avoided being buried by falling masonry. All of us could say: *there but for the grace of God go I.*

I knew many of those working for Canterbury TV where 115 dead lay amidst smoldering rubble. I went to the CTV studios at least once a week for interviews. I could have been there that day; at that time.

People's bravery was astounding. Immediately after buildings crumbled, many people ignored dangers caused by aftershocks and ran into rubble to rescue victims.

One of those brave souls was one of our own: Joe Pohio. Joe was a very popular Council worker. He ran the social club.

He was in the central city when shop frontages collapsed around him. Many people panicked and fled, but Joe did not. He rushed to a woman, screaming in pain, who was trapped under masonry. Frantically, Joe tried to lift the stones and slabs off her.

Another aftershock struck. Joe looked up and saw the wall of the building coming towards them. He threw himself over the woman to protect her. The collapsed wall killed him.

Joe's death highlights a terrible thing about earthquakes. It is the randomness, the madness, of it all. Nobody is safe.

Heroism occurred all over town. Many ordinary people burrowed into the rubble, disregarding the considerable risk to their own well-being. Julian Shah, a doctor from King Edward V11's Hospital, London, was one. In Christchurch to speak at a urological conference, he risked his life when he helped rescue a woman trapped on the top floor of The Press building, home of the city's morning newspaper.

To reach her, Dr Shah crawled on hands and knees through the rubble of the building's top two stories. He treated the seriously injured woman until she was freed by a crane. When he tried to escape, he found the stairs demolished by an aftershock. To reach safety, he jumped across a gaping chasm, four floors deep, to reach the roof of an adjoining building.

Two other doctors, Bryce Curran, an anesthetist at Christchurch Hospital, and Lydia Putra, an Australian urologist, used a pocket knife and a hacksaw to amputate the legs of a man trapped under beams in the PGC building. The woman doctor had found the man after she crawled through rubble for more than five hours searching for survivors.

She was very brave. Aftershocks caused huge concrete beams hovering over her to move throughout her search. She was lucky to get out alive.

A nurse, Andrea Robinson, helped injured at the Palms Mall and performed CPR on a cyclist whose back was broken.
Similar acts of heroism occurred all over town. Christchurch Hospital, which was partially closed because of damage, treated nearly 7,000 people injured in the earthquake. More than 200 were serious trauma cases.

Ashley Vickers, from Linwood, showed great presence of mind when he saw a mother and her daughter trapped in a badly damaged building in Kilmore Street. He grabbed a ladder from a nearby contractor and, despite continuing aftershocks and the possibility of the building collapsing, Ashley climbed up and rescued them.

Murray Straight, from Templeton, reacted with similar courage when he noticed a woman trapped on the first floor of the Link Centre between Hereford Street and City Mall. He found a ladder in a nearby shop and, ignoring the threats posed by aftershocks, climbed up the side of the damaged building. He smashed a window and helped 15 people down to safety.

Erwin Polczak used his hands, a broom and a crowbar to dig four people from underneath rubble outside the OK Gift Shop in the city centre. It was extremely dangerous work. He burrowed under rubble and was squeezed as the rubble shifted with aftershocks.

On the days following the earthquake, he worked as a civilian volunteer, delivering food to other rescuers toiling in the Red Zone.

Chris Nutsford, an experienced rock climber, offered his services to firemen searching for survivors at the PGC building. He climbed on the building and rescued three women from a toilet block on the third floor. Concrete beams loosened by aftershocks posed a constant threat as he toiled to free the women.

Blair Corkran had just bought his lunch at a bakery in Cashel Mall when the earthquake struck. He rescued several people, including a baby, and stayed with one of the seriously injured bakery staff, Shane Tomlinson, who sadly died.

I fretted for my own family's safety. It was after midnight before I learned they were safe and unharmed.

I often went to Latimer Square to visit Urban Search and Rescue teams (USARs). It was like being at the United Nations. Apart from our own people, who were there within hours of the earthquake, teams came from all around the world. Four hundred and thirty nine people from seven countries – United Kingdom, Australia, United States of America, Japan, China, Taiwan and Singapore.

Australia had a team of 72 there within 12 hours of the earthquake. American and Singaporean USAR teams arrived within two days. Another 70 arrived from Queensland with dogs for the grisly task of locating bodies.

The USARs were brave beyond belief. Few people would volunteer to undertake the risks they accepted as a matter of course.

Paul Burns, leader of the Christchurch USAR team was preparing to play golf when the earthquake struck. He returned home to check on the safety of his family and neighbours and managed to telephone his superiors in Wellington from a landline in his house.

Stuart Black, the USAR Special Operations Manager was in a meeting and unavailable. Paul suggested the secretary inform Mr Black that Paul was mobilising his Christchurch team because there had been another major earthquake. He suggested they place two North Island teams on standby.

He then drove to the USAR base behind the Woolston Fire Brigade. Although it suffered no structural damage, it was covered in liquefaction. Communications were down and he could not contact other members of the team.

Paul tried to drive into the city, but traffic gridlocked. Texts requesting assistance and painting a dire picture of the extent of damage kept coming through on his cell phone. It took two hours to get into town. Other USAR members battled for five hours to get there, all the time conscious that people trapped in buildings needed their help.

The USAR worldwide network is such that other teams around the globe knew within minutes that Christchurch had suffered another devastating earthquake. Offers of assistance immediately arrived via a United Nations website specifically established for such events.

Simple messages appeared on computer screens: USA – am available. Australia – am available. Japan – am available. Britain – am available.

Others texted contacts within New Zealand's USAR teams and asked: *Do you want a hand?*

Within a couple of hours of the earthquake, Paul informed his superiors in Wellington, they would require the international help offered. He was appointed On Site Operations Co-ordination Centre manager, responsible for all the USAR teams that eventually moved onto a base established at Latimer Square.

As with the rest of the civil defence team, information about which buildings had collapsed was difficult to obtain because communications were so difficult. Initially, USARs, too, relied on media reports to direct them to rescue sites.

Paul sent a team to the Cathedral after being told tourists were trapped inside. USARs withdrew from there when an aftershock tore down more of the stone building. They decided it was too dangerous.

They diverted to The Press building nearby and rescued five people.

Paul deployed 15 tonnes of rescue equipment to damaged buildings throughout the city. The demand for it was such that he had to prioritise where it went. Equipment included concrete cutting chainsaws, listening devices to locate people, airbags and 25 tonne and 50 tonne jacks for lifting concrete slab beams.

They worked urgently, diligently, with the knowledge that, in disasters such as this, most rescues occur within the first seven hours. As time went on, rescues became less frequent and more difficult. Rescuers climbed into cavities and squeezed under beams, calling, tapping and looking for signs of life. Initially, it was easy to identify victims' whereabouts because they were able to indicate where they were. It became more difficult with time.

Within a few hours, firefighters and USAR team members were combing the rubble of the CTV building, the PGC building, The Press building, Colombo and Manchester Streets and every other badly damaged site where victims might lie. Two USAR teams arrived from the North Island at 10:30pm and relieved those who had toiled throughout the afternoon and evening.

Firemen had little rest. Shortly after arriving at Latimer Square, they were sent to fight a fire in a supermarket in Colombo Street.

Within a couple of hours of the earthquake, Andrew Scipione, Commissioner of Police in New South Wales, Australia, was offering assistance to his New Zealand equivalent Harold Broad.

Three hundred and fifty three police came from Australia. They were sworn in as temporary constables in the New Zealand Police Force. They worked alongside their New Zealand colleagues, manning barricades, assisting with search and rescue, searching for missing people, gathering evidence about fatalities and helping Disaster Victim Identification (DVI) teams. Five countries provided 40 specialists in disaster identification.

Relationships between the two countries' police have always been strong. They regularly work together on extraditions, criminal investigations and training. New Zealand police carried out victim identification during Australian bushfires. The countries' police had worked together in Thailand after the 2004 Boxing Day tsunami as well as in east Timor, Bougainville and Afghanistan.

Australian police were overwhelmed by the reception they received in Christchurch. They received standing ovations when arriving and departing Christchurch International Airport. It was such a far cry from the sometimes boorish behaviour their sporting teams can receive when in this city.

One hardened Australian policeman was so overwhelmed by spontaneous outbursts of gratitude that he admitted to crying with emotion on three occasions. He had never reacted that way before.

Everyone worked tirelessly in dangerous, dirty conditions.

Australia also sent a 75 bed field hospital which was set up in the eastern suburbs. It provided many of the services available at base hospitals around the country.

Jo and I were at the PGC building when the last survivor, Ann Bodkin, was pulled from the rubble. I was travelling into the Red Zone with a group of journalists. I jumped off at the PGC building and noticed a man standing nearby, all alone.

Graham Richardson revealed it was his partner that rescuers were trying to save.

While we talked, I received a call that the 26 storey Grand Chancellor Hotel could topple. Jo volunteered to stay with Graham while I went to the hotel to assist in clearing media away.

The Grand Chancellor, a five star hotel, was Christchurch's tallest building. Ironically, it had survived the 7.1 magnitude earthquake in September without any apparent damage. This earthquake had caused it to drop by a metre on one side. We feared that if it collapsed, it could cause its own earthquake, and fell other surrounding buildings. If on-lookers were too close, they would be injured. We had to get them to safety. We evacuated a two block area around the hotel.

Meanwhile, Jo watched as rescuers, working from ladders, and inside the rubble, tried to reach Ann. When the quake struck, Ann had dived under a desk for protection. She was trapped in that confined space beneath tonnes of rubble for 26 hours. Throughout her ordeal, the earth had shaken and jolted and rolled with aftershocks. Neither she nor rescuers were confident the tremors would not bring everything down upon them.

The aftershocks were almost constant: relentless, merciless. Unless you were there, you would not believe how many there were. Often, the earth rolled beneath our feet, giving us a sensation of being aboard a ship in heavy seas.

Ann was very lucky to be found. An Australian TV journalist had heard her cries for help and alerted rescuers that somebody was still alive in the building. Until then, Graham had had no idea where she was. He had searched hospitals and other places, and checked lists of deceased until rescuers summoned him to the PGC building because Ann was asking for him.

Applause greeted Ann, wrapped in a blanket and wearing a neck brace, as she was carried on a stretcher from her concrete tomb. She was the last person brought out alive.

Within 48 hours of the earthquake it was obvious that probably everyone buried in the rubble was dead. Although rescuers knew it was a fruitless exercise, they continued to drop into voids and squeeze through the tightest of spaces in futile attempts to find another person alive.

We were approaching a point at which we would have to make the dreadful call that the operation would move from one of rescuing people to one of recovering bodies.

Search conditions were particularly arduous in the CTV building where rescuers had to contend with dangers posed by fire, as well as the collapsed building. Smoke made it impossible to remain in voids in which they would normally search. They had little water to douse the fire.

The decision would be made collectively. Obviously, police and civil defence and Government would have significant input.

The transition from rescue to recovery would change our modus operandi. Until now, USARs had combed the city, around the clock, desperately searching for survivors.

Triage stations had been set up in Latimer Square, along with a temporary morgue. Grieving families congregated outside, waiting to identify their loved ones.

Some mornings, I snatched a break from fielding media questions and went there and sat in the cold to offer what little comfort I could. Naturally, people were terribly upset.

One morning, I saw a familiar figure in the throng at Latimer Square. It was my son, Dan, a journalist with TV3. He had arrived from Wellington. We threw our arms around each other and hugged and cried. Apart from Jo, he was my first physical contact with my family since this horrible ordeal began.

Timing for switching the operation from rescue to recovery involved the EOC team in lengthy debate. Although we doubted we would find survivors, relatives naturally clung to hope. They would be devastated and sceptical if we made our decision too soon.

Because of this, and the strong desire to find survivors, we probably waited longer than was necessary before making the announcement. Mr. Hamilton announced the change in status on 3 March 2011. He pointed out that 70 people had been rescued but nobody had been brought out alive since 23 February.

"We now face the reality that there is no chance that anyone could have survived this long," he announced.

The missing included 28 Japanese English language students who, at 12:51pm that fateful Tuesday afternoon, were at a school inside the CTV building.

Japan sent its own USAR team to recover those youthful bodies. They arrived just before Mr Hamilton's announcement. I watched as the team searched the ashes and the detritus of the CTV building.

They worked every hour of every day. Each team worked a six

hour shift. They were brave, dedicated people who followed strict protocols.

At the end of each shift, a new squad, dressed in pristine uniforms, would assemble at Latimer Square. Looking immaculate, the visors on their helmets catching the sun, or floodlights at night, they would march the short distance to the CTV building. With military precision, they would come to a halt, turn and face the building and their comrades who were lined up to come out of the rubble after completing their six hours of sifting and crawling through the ruins for traces of the students.

In contrast to the new arrivals' clean appearance, the shift leaving the site would be bedraggled. Their uniforms, spotless six hours previously, were torn and covered in dirt, soot and grime. Physically exhausted, they would line up, hold their heads high, and march to Latimer Square.

Every time they retrieved a body, or part of one, they would lift it so gently, with immense dignity, and carry it to a stretcher on the street. They would form a circle around the remains of a young Japanese student and pray.

I have never seen physical actions in such a hostile environment undertaken in such a beautiful, spiritual, respectful manner. You could feel their dignity, strength, courage and pain.

When they left Christchurch, they did not know that they were going to deal with something much more horrific, and on a much more terrifying scale, than they had encountered here. They returned home to the nightmare of the catastrophic 8.9 magnitude earthquake and tsunami that devastated northern Japan on 11 March 2011.

Members of other USAR teams that worked at Christchurch followed them there, including some of our own. When the USARs departed, they left behind a legacy of courage and tirelessness that will never be forgotten by the people of Christchurch.

The Americans also left behind all of the rescue equipment they had brought here. Little did they suspect that our USAR team would, within days of receiving the gift, ship it to Japan for use there.

In a message the US Secretary of State, Hillary Clinton, sent to the Memorial Service to commemorate the first anniversary of the Christchurch earthquake, she made special mention of the USARs' contribution. She said:

> *In the aftermath of the earthquake the United States, along with many other countries, sent an Urban Search and Rescue Team to provide assistance. When their mission ended, the US team gave their advanced rescue equipment to their Kiwi partners so the work could continue.*
>
> *When earthquakes struck Japan, just weeks later, New Zealand quickly deployed its own teams along with that same equipment. In America, we call that "paying it forward". And it was international relations at its very best.*
>
> *Even those of us who were far away on that terrible day share in your grief, and we know it's been a struggle, but through that struggle, we've seen the strength and perseverance of the people of Christchurch.*

While the spotlight fell on USAR teams that removed rubble to retrieve bodies, another group toiled with little recognition. They were the Land Search and Rescue (LanSAR) units. They were comprised of young men and women, volunteers, who arrived from all over the South Island, and much of the North as well.

Usually, they work on a regional basis, rescuing and recovering trampers lost in the bush, or victims of accidents, in their areas.

I must admit, I had not heard of them before.

Someone came into the Art Gallery expressing concern that all these volunteers were being ignored. They suggested I should visit them. Jo, Di Keenan, our communications manager, and I headed out to Halswell Domain where the LanSARs were based. We found an encampment of hundreds of men and women from mainly rural towns throughout New Zealand. They had set up a mobile command centre in the Domain hall. I jumped onto a platform and gave a short speech in which I sincerely thanked them for the vital work they were doing.

The LanSARs were actually making a huge contribution. They carefully walked the whole of the Peninsula, and checked out 60,000 houses around the city.

Extraordinary geological events took place on hills dividing the city from the Peninsula. Cliffs collapsed and houses tumbled down their sides. Several people walking the hills on that beautiful summer day died.

The earthquake's force was such that it catapulted rocks weighing several tonnes out of the earth. Its energy was so intense that it shot the boulders vertically into the air at an incredible velocity. Rocks did not fall because they were shaken from cliffs. They were actually shot out like cannon balls.

Unlike boulders, the projectiles were not round. They comprised odd shapes and sizes. Some were as big as picnic baskets; others the size of small trucks. On striking the ground, they shattered into a dozen or more fragments.

These pieces then set off themselves, spinning, in different directions. They were not round and smooth. They had sharp, flat edges. They spun down the hillsides like buzz saws, cutting through wire fences and felling trees. It was an extraordinary and frightening phenomena which scientists had not seen before. They uncovered the earthquake's vicious secret through studying the ruts and furrows nature's missiles embedded in the Port Hills.

Mr Key and I flew over the hills on 23 February when inspecting the extent of the city's devastation. We left from Hagley Park, which had been turned into a mini-airport with perhaps half a dozen helicopters at a time using it. It even had its own air traffic controller.

First, we flew over Christchurch city. Liquefaction covered vast parts of the eastern suburbs like a flood. Water still pumped out of the ground faster than it could drain away.

Mr Key was interested in conditions at the Port Hills because he had a relative living at Mt Pleasant. From a distance, houses nestling on the hills looked sound. However, the closer we approached, the worse the devastation became. The immense energy force that had propelled the huge boulders from the ground had blasted tiles from roofs and exploded bricks off walls and onto lawns. Nature's energy had pushed up the Port Hills themselves so that today they are nearly one metre higher than they were on the morning of 22 February.

"This is not the Christchurch we knew," Mr Key observed, "it is closer to a war zone."

It was true. The city appeared to have been under a sustained rocket and artillery attack. From our vantage point in the helicopter, we noticed that aftershocks were continuing under the ground below. Each aftershock caused dust to billow where dislodged boulders landed. It was like a bombardment. It continued relentlessly for weeks.

From the September earthquake, we learnt how important human contact is during a disaster, for almost everyone, regardless of whether their houses are damaged. Everyone on the Peninsula and throughout Christchurch had experienced a catastrophic earthquake; they were all shaken emotionally, and they all had a story they needed to tell. Sharing their experiences, fears and hopes with someone else seemed to provide a degree of relief.

That was one of the primary roles the LanSARs filled. They provided an ear for listening to the stories and concerns of thousands of earthquake survivors. They also offered a kind word, a word of encouragement, or advice, about how to deal with problems. We told the LanSARs to bang on doors and let people know assistance was available, even if they did not require it. Naturally, the process uncovered people who did need help but had not sought it.

We also requested that LanSARs should conduct a quick external assessment of the state of properties they visited. Because they called at so many houses, they saw how bad conditions actually were and gathered threads of information which, when we received it, we added to the tapestry of chaos being stitched together by EOC at the Art Gallery.

Jo and I fell into a routine of taking a LOV into the suburbs every day to buoy spirits of LanSARs, volunteers, and residents. We met remarkable people and heard incredible stories about close calls and escapes from death. There was also much heartbreak. One graphic account of the quake's shock waves rolling into the east of the city was astonishing. A man recounted what had happened while he sat in a bus shelter on one of the main eastern arterial roads, at 12:51pm 22 February.

He was nonchalantly browsing through a copy of The Press while waiting for a bus to arrive. A deep, low, rumble that we have all learnt precedes the arrival of an earthquake caught his attention. He could not believe what he saw.

Waves in the ground advanced toward him, at high speed, from the direction in which he thought the rumble emanated.

The road tarmac rose and fell like the ocean. Vehicles veered, often completely off the road, as the waves lifted them. Manhole covers rose up and burst open. Power poles lurched from side to side like yacht masts in a storm. Stunned, he sat there, holding his newspaper, watching in disbelief.

The waves struck the bus shelter. Its glass panels flexed and shattered, showering him with fragments. His feet remained planted firmly on the ground as he braced himself against the violent movement.

He felt something on his feet. Water gushed out of the ground, as if a huge spring had opened up beneath him. Within seconds, black water covered the street. It rose over his ankles, eventually up to his knees.

He decided to return home. His journey became more perilous with each step. He stumbled into sinkholes that were hidden under the black sludge. Some were so big they swallowed cars.

By the time he reached home, water was up to his thighs. He was covered in mud and soaking wet. Wading up his driveway, he became even more perturbed. Water lapped about his front door. On opening the door, he found springs bubbling through the floor boards.

His story was common to thousands of residents, particularly in the eastern suburbs.

This seismic tide ran for several days. Every aftershock caused sand volcanoes which, each time, gouged more water out of the ground.

When the tide receded, it left thousands of houses filled with mud. Sections were buried under it. Drains were blocked and pipes broken. It was the most miserable, awful, experience.

One cannot witness people's plights without feeling it one's self, particularly in the circumstances in which Cantabrians languished. The sense of loss, confusion and trauma they carried in their souls was etched on their faces and reflected through their eyes. We could not help but feel it. We saw it when we looked them in the eyes. We felt it when we shook their hands, or when we gave each other hugs. Often, we would feel their tears on our cheeks. It was a very emotional time.

Sometimes, the stories they heard, and the sights they saw, drove staff accompanying us to disappear from view to weep. Jo and I were determined our emotions would not leak in public. Our job was to lift spirits, to give hope and reassurance; to remind them that, no matter how dark the day might be, storms always pass and the sun always shines again. Jo and I were together all the time and we supported each other through the emotion of it all. I could not have done it alone.

We reiterated to people that we were all in this together and, together, we would rebuild and create a future that would be better than the past. In the meantime, could we do anything to help? Did they have a portaloo? A chemical toilet? Water? Food? Were they warm enough? How had neighbours and other family members fared?

Even when people wrapped their arms around me and pressed my broken ribs, I was determined not to flinch or whimper in front of them. The truth was, I needed their love as much as they needed mine.

I quickly identified unexpected little things that could help them come to terms with their emotions and reactions. Honesty and humility were virtues that worked like angels dispensing blessings. People often asked how I had felt during the earthquake. I admitted to being frightened. They looked relieved that I bared my heart and revealed my frailties; often, they confessed that they, too, had known fear. Our honesty became our bond.

Some people, though, were angry and vented their frustration. I was prepared to accept their ire. I was determined

I should not respond angrily myself, although occasionally, I felt I had every right to. I felt that as Mayor, people felt the buck stopped with me; and, that they were justified in their belief, because it does, anyway.

The austerity we all experienced brought out the best and the worst qualities in people. It highlighted deficiencies that we, as a society, have created, despite our best intentions. The earthquake re-enforced that our society has created people who are dependent upon others for almost everything. It is one of the inevitabilities of life. Having deprived these folks of the skills to cope in good times, how do we expect them to perform during a catastrophe?

This became apparent during the State of Emergency. Some people could not cope, particularly those who had relied on welfare for a long time. They found the fractured social and support structures that followed the earthquake very difficult to accept.

Suddenly, during a catastrophe, all their supports disappeared. Everyone, without exception, experiences significant gaps in their lives. For those who lack self-reliance and commonsense, life becomes that much harder. They cannot cope.

We learned this lesson during the September quake. Therefore, the second time around, we knew where the pressure points would arise, and what the issues would be.

These people do not have internet and are often lacking social skill sets. Many have travelled a hard road.

In many cases the most vulnerable people in our community were least able to cope with the disaster. They were enmeshed in a system in which somebody always solved a problem for them.

On the other hand, we discovered much more self sufficiency than dependence. Every community contains people who stepped up to become leaders, and people's generosity and ingenuity continuously inspired us. Leaders came forward and began to organise others. Often, they saw gaps in the system that we could not see.

CanCERN was such an organisation. Set up by Tom McBrearty, it went door-to-door to check on people. It held community meetings at which it identified residents' problems and reported them to us. It let us know when there were not enough portaloos in a street, or if there were leaks in houses which created heating problems for residents.

Initially, we feared CanCERN was little more than a politically motivated pressure group. The reality was that it became increasingly adept at articulating the real needs and concerns of local communities. We quickly realised that because civil defence had insufficient people on the ground, CanCERN could be an ally.

Tom and the team he built around him proved to be exactly that. This grass roots organisation demonstrated the strength of a community based response to the 22 February earthquake. In the months ahead we learnt to work closely with them. It was a valuable lesson. It has changed the way I view the contribution local groups can make in helping to manage a disaster.

The lesson we learned was that the sooner we empower and support a local community response, as opposed to a centrally driven civil defence response, the sooner that community will begin to recover.

John Leonard, the Principal at Freeville School, North New Brighton, was another example of grass roots driven community support. He organised jackets, gumboots and warm clothes for families. He organised the provision of food parcels, counselling, and financial support and established a regular information flow that updated residents on the situation prevailing in Christchurch.

Also at North New Brighton, James Ridpath and members

of the Youth Alive Trust organised fun events for schoolchildren. Their objective was to provide a sense of normality and enjoyment for children struggling to cope with ongoing aftershocks. Many of their homes had been badly damaged by earthquakes. The Trust took 85 children to Auckland for a holiday away from aftershocks.

On the other side of town, at Addington, Mike Peters formed Addington Action, a community group that provides assistance to local residents. It has helped more than 500 people with food, toilet facilities, water and repairs.

Zhihong Lu worked with the Chinese community at Riccarton. Translating messages from Civil Defence proved to be particularly beneficial.

Chris Crowe, of Cashmere, established the Canterbury Quake Live website *(www.canterburyquakelive.co.nz)*. It provided information about the earthquake and ongoing aftershocks.

Melanie Hiller, of Aranui, without power or water connected to her home, organised 260 meals a day for distribution to the needy. She managed this by collecting water and getting a generator from Ashburton.

Melanie extended her services by distributing secondhand clothing and furniture to people who had lost their's in the earthquakes. She also brought joy to the suburb's children by arranging a "Quake Escape" to Hanmer Springs and Little River.

The importance of communication, and how it played out in a disaster was another valuable lesson we learnt from the 4 September earthquake. If people know the facts, then they will accept the reasons why something cannot happen. But keep them in the dark, deprive them of information, and frustration and anger boil to the surface.

Obviously, conveying information to people during a disaster can be extremely difficult. Because there is no electricity, there is no TV, which is a prime source of many people's knowledge. Without power, radio is also unavailable to many people. They lost broadband connections, which denied them opportunities for accessing information from the internet, and they could not recharge the batteries on phones, another essential information vehicle.

We urged the public to engage their minds; for instance, if they had a car, they probably had a radio in it. We asked them to sit in their cars and listen to updates on their situation. Cars became a safety cell from where people could glean knowledge for survival.

From their radios they learned where they could get fresh, clean water. They heard about community services they could tap into. They received weather forecasts, learned which roads were accessible, and progress on restoring electricity. They found out how they should deal with human waste and what action they should take to avoid the looming threat of spreading disease.

After 22 February, we responded quickly – within a week – by holding public meetings. Our challenge was how to tell people without access to the usual communications vehicles the time, date and location of meetings.

We reverted to old fashioned methods: we stuck fliers on lamp posts, dropped notices into letterboxes, told people to get out and meet each other, to talk to each other, and to establish their own information networks.

Water distribution centres – usually tankers parked strategically around suburbs, or pipes connected to boreholes and springs – became popular venues for sharing news, frustrations and gossip. People chatted to each other while queuing to fill bottles, buckets and plastic containers.

We sent an advance team into the suburbs to erect loudspeakers and a podium in spaces safe for groups to gather. To address meetings, they took a cross-section of people from the Council, EQC, Orion (an electricity provider), police and any others deemed appropriate, to explain issues and answer questions.

Residents gave us feedback and made suggestions which were enormously helpful.

Those attending the meetings lived in dire circumstances. Many were traumatized from their experiences. Most treated us well and genuinely appreciated the efforts we made to supply information.

Sewage was a major concern. Pipes broke and clogged with silt from liquefaction, causing widespread damage in the city and eastern suburbs. For a while, people had to dig holes in their backyards to dispose of waste.

As we have seen repeatedly in Canterbury, rather than allow this hardship to break their spirits, people endeavoured to have fun with it. Social media, Facebook, YouTube and Twitter have helped with this. People used them to share information and find humour in the midst of all this. Humour is one of the parts of the human emotional make-up, which is absolutely vital for survival. People's ability to turn the mundane and necessary into fun was incredible.

Humour happened spontaneously. Someone set up a website with a picture of their long drop (outdoor latrine). The concept of building creative latrines in the backyard became a source of pride as residents sought to be more imaginative than neighbours. My father built a most elaborate long drop. It had a window and a transistor radio in it. Humour was essential in beating adversity.

The same thing happened with the orange cones that dominate our streets. Prior to the Memorial Service an Internet campaign encouraged flowers be placed on the cones as if we could turn the symbol of our destruction into fun.

Civil Defence provided portaloos to help with sanitation

and to stop waste leaching into streams, rivers and storm water systems. It was intended they should be placed in every street where sewer pipes were broken. Unfortunately, many of the portaloos ended up in streets that did not need them, while those that did, missed out.

The whole issue flared to become one of the major irritants of the State of Emergency. It reflected badly on the Council, when, in reality, it was not of its making. With better communication and an understanding of the local communities involved, the problem would not have arisen. I sympathised with people's frustrations.

In my opinion, the problem arose because the National Civil Defence command took responsibility for distributing portaloos. If they had used local resources, such as volunteer fire brigades, to decide where they should be placed, distribution would have proceeded much more effectively. Community based groups are acutely aware of local requirements. They would have known exactly where the portaloos should be placed. Wellington bureaucrats lacked that information.

Civil defence acted in good faith, but in ignorance. John Hamilton was told portaloos had been delivered to areas at which they had not arrived. When challenged by media, his records showed they had been delivered. TV footage showed that, clearly, they had not. Irate residents condemned the Council on TV.

For a start, although we had taken delivery of every portaloo we could locate on the planet, we did not have enough. We ordered almost 1000 portaloos and 40,000 chemical toilets. Some came from the USA, others came from China and other countries.

Public ire over the portaloo issue was not indicative of the public's mood. Generally, people were tremendous. The reaction to our meetings, and when we visited suburbs, was often overwhelming. I would thank those attending, and compliment them on how resolute they were. I would apologise that we may not have reacted as fast as they would like in some instances, and explained the importance of receiving their feedback and how it had enabled us to identify and rectify problems. Generally, the messages were well received.

Not everybody, though, was complimentary. I was deeply hurt to be called a racist because I had not visited a particular marae, and was perceived to be spending too much time in more affluent suburbs.

That was insulting and ridiculous. There was no favouritism for any parts of the city. The criticism came from someone closely aligned to the Labour Party. I find it disgusting that some on the political left used the adversity the city faced for scoring cheap shots to gain political support.

On the other hand, we saw many people, particularly the elderly, rise above the dire circumstances in which they found themselves. Here we were, a First World country, reduced in only a few seconds to living in the most basic of Third World conditions.

So many people had lost their homes. I had to be frank: I had no inkling about how long it would take to resolve their problems. Undoubtedly, it would take an awfully long time.

Many times I wondered how people coped with the circumstances in which they found themselves; many had lost everything and were too old to start again.

Amidst the carnage, people, especially the elderly, frequently surprised us with their generosity and kindness.

"Don't worry about us," they would say. "We'll be fine."

We heard that refrain repeated time and again.

They would tell us to worry, instead, about some "old dear" down the road.

"Lots of people have got more to worry about than us. Our children have all grown up and gone away…"

People humbled me with their ability to minimise their own predicaments. Often these folk had lived in their houses for decades, even generations; their houses were their whole lives. Despite the damage, the pride with which their homes were maintained was often still apparent, even though they were in ruins, or askew, or full of liquefaction and uninhabitable. Their homes still reflected their pride and their personalities through little things. It was touching to see flowers blooming in a garden in a street transformed to resemble a lunar landscape by tonnes of grey sludge. It was far removed from the *Garden City* of which we had been so proud. Inside, photographs and trinkets lay strewn across floors. There was little point returning these treasures to walls and cabinets; they were likely to come down again with the next aftershock.

They had all worked hard for their homes. For many, their houses were their saving's nest egg for retirement. Now, it was gone.

Time and again, I was reminded about how cruel life can be.

Despite all the hardship, people remained kind. I would walk up a driveway to deliver food and be greeted with a smile, a firm hand, and an offer of a cup of tea.

Nothing abnormal about that? Only their hardship. Their house was askew and filled with liquefaction. They had no running water. Their toilet was a hole in the ground. They had been robbed of their futures and the certainty they thought they had about life. In an instant they had lost everything. They had no idea what the future held. How do you deal with that? Anger? Rage? Remarkably, somehow, they managed to remain civil. I found it extraordinary.

Frequently, these visits reminded me of my parent's predicament. Their house was badly bashed about. I felt guilty for their suffering and that I could not be there to support them. It used to rip my heart out.

Just as heartbreaking, though, were people in the suburbs. One woman, in particular, lingers in my mind. We came across her when delivering food with the army. She was in her 90s. Her house was broken and twisted. A vegetable patch had obviously been her pride and joy. She had removed liquefaction from the base of tomato plants.

"Don't worry about me," she said, "I've got it good. I can live in this house. I'm not going to be around much longer, so there is no point in rebuilding my house."

She was delighted that the student army, the thousands of young people who spontaneously pitched in to clear liquefaction from streets, gutters and sections, were clearing her yard.

"I just want to get the dirt off the garden and get the plants growing again," she said.

Sadly, her house was given a red sticker which meant that, despite her determination, she would have to leave.

You cannot fail to be moved by that sort of personal humility and strength. It has moved me many times.

Such incidents made our personal hardships easier to bear. We usually got home at about 11pm. We worked ourselves to the bone. Hour-after-hour, week-after-week. We would return home to a place that offered us little more than a bed on which to lie. Like thousands of others, we had no water, no shower, no sewerage, and no electricity. As tired as we were, continuing aftershocks robbed us of sleep. As with everyone else in Christchurch, we would lie in bed listening to the quakes coming. We would catch our breath and wait to see how severe they were. We waited to see if we would survive. Even now, it continues.

We had only one proper shower during the first couple of

weeks after 22 February, when the Deputy Mayor, Ngaire Button, invited us to her house which had water trickling through taps. Apart from that, we brought bottled water home, heated it on a gas burner, and had a flannel wash every day. Initially, that was the only water we could get. Any that was left over from washing, we tipped into the cistern which enabled us to flush the toilet once. However, even that basic necessity was not immediately available because the sewer was broken and could not be used.

After a week, or so, we noticed a trickle of water coming through the taps. It was insufficient to fill a hot water tank and turn the heater on, but it was enough for a skimpy shower if we did not mind getting cold in the process. That was a significant step forward.

Then, one day, the lavatory cistern filled with water, all on its own. Suddenly, we could flush the toilet. But we were allowed to flush it only twice a day because that was all the pipes could handle. However, it provided a significant improvement to our lives. It demonstrated that luxury, like beauty, truly is a matter of perception.

On any given day in a city the size of Christchurch, hundreds of people are lonely. Unfortunately, loneliness is prevalent in our society today. The lonely linger in shops, just to see another human being. They long to hear another voice, a giggle, laughter, or even a sneeze or a cough.

Because their loneliness embarrasses them, they hide their malady with a smile, and display a brave face. Then they return home. They have nobody there. They sit on their own for hours until the sun goes down. They go to sleep, and get up and go out for a while again the next day. Their contact with other humans is minimal.

Can you imagine what it was like for the lonely when the earthquakes ripped the city apart? They had nobody to call. Neither did they have anyone to reassure or comfort them. No one cared whether they were okay.

Aware of this, I went on air whenever I could and said: "Each one of you is important, more important than any of us here in the Emergency Operations Centre. You've got to go and check on your neighbours. You've got to help people, because we can't do it all. We are not going to be able to go everywhere. It is going to take us some days to get out to where you are to start repairing and providing services.

"We are getting water tankers. We are bringing in toilets. We've got some showers coming. We are distributing food. But you are going to have to make sure that the person in the house next door, who you may never have talked to before, is okay. You could do that, because we can't do that yet."

And people did that.

People, particularly the elderly, realised they were not alone.

It was a clarion call that catapulted a human tsunami of volunteers, the spontaneity of which New Zealand had not seen for a long time. Many people were surprised. They detected a new spirit, a new selfless attitude, blooming in the community.

I do not believe that it was, in fact, a seismic shift in attitude. It was more a kind of self empowerment, or reawakening of the human spirit. That caring nature has always been there. I believe a human being's basic instinct is to help people in need.

While this virtue lies within us all, it has been usurped by materialism. However, given certain circumstances, compassion and that desire to help our neighbour rises to the surface and becomes compelling. Evidence of that occurred, time and again, in Christchurch. It continues to do so today.

In local government, we get to see both the worst and the best of human nature. We see many people who are deeply involved in helping others. It is a positive aspect of belonging to a community.

Some people help all the time. In rural areas, where I began my career in local government, people will, to this day, mend things themselves if you give them the nails and wood. They prefer to repair something themselves, rather than have the Council do it.

When I moved to Banks Peninsula over 22 years ago, there was no difficulty getting people to mow the grass at reserves. In fact, it happened spontaneously all around the Peninsula. It continues to happen in these rural areas, but not generally in the city. Society has become more selfish and more obsessed with materialism. The purpose of life has become, in many cases, to build a comfortable nest, and to enjoy one's self.

This is a comparatively recent phenomenon. It did not dominate past generations to the extent it does contemporary society. Thirty years ago there was no problem getting volunteers. There is today.

While previous generations were concerned about attaining a good standard of living, they did not forget that communities were cooperative entities which comprised all sorts of connections. They interacted by talking to each other. Today, with social media, we interact in a different, more isolated, way.

Elderly people I met in the suburbs demonstrated the attitudinal shift that has occurred between generations. Many of them, like my parents, have never had a mortgage. They were taught that you should not buy something until you had enough cash for the purchase. They scrimped and saved and equipped themselves with skills to get by; skills that, today, unfortunately, are difficult to find. They were self sufficient. They adopted simple techniques to provide for themselves, for example through bottling preserves, growing their own vegetables, baking, and creating their own fun. They developed an instinct for survival.

They were of stock that many of us feel was remarkable – they are the generation of the Great Depression and the Second World War. The hardship and sacrifice of these times instilled within them a strong sense of community spirit.

Reflecting on the impact of events in London during the Second World War, regardless of how many bombs Hitler dropped on the city, the bombardment had an opposite impact than expected. It actually made people stronger.

Here, in Christchurch, the physiological and psychological assaults on citizens, from literally thousands of earthquakes, has not been dissimilar to that endured by those brave souls who weathered the Battle of Britain. A parallel can also be drawn to the way in which Cantabrians have reacted. We will not be beaten. We have discovered an inner strength to help each other through these difficult, challenging, times.

Our dire circumstances triggered qualities that lay inert inside us all.

The difference, after the earthquakes, is that, previously, only small groups had cared for their communities; now, it is everyone. Anyone who was able to make a contribution, whether it was cleaning up liquefaction, or providing food and companionship, or numerous other tasks, large and small, did something.

Thousands of people shed their inhibitions, jealousies, resentments and selfishness, and rolled up their sleeves, put on their working clothes, and got stuck in to make a difference.

That is how the earthquakes changed people. The quakes enabled them to respond spontaneously, from their hearts.

An earthquake is an incredibly random event. It is not going to occur at a predicted time or place; its effects do not follow a consistent pattern – one building is fine, the next has fallen down; another has people trapped in it; others do not. The event hits without warning. The scale of destruction can vary for reasons beyond our understanding. And there is the randomness to those who are injured and those who die. It is just like war.

All those war stories that we see nightly on TV, happening somewhere else – people being burnt, buildings being blown up – an earthquake is just like that.

The severity, frequency and nature of the earthquakes gave people the equivalent of a war time experience. It caused seismic activity far beyond the land – it shook hearts and minds and caused a very strong psychological shift in Canterbury. Perhaps, it could be one of the blessings to emerge from the tragedy.

When a community has contemplated the possibility of dying, on more than one occasion, its values change. What was our first reaction after confronting death? For many of us, we desperately needed to know our children's whereabouts. We telephoned our children, our parents, our partner, our loved ones. We did not telephone the bank manager or publican to see if they were okay.

We wondered about our extended family and friends. Were they safe? Where were they? What had they lost? Those connections became much stronger because we had contemplated the possibility of losing them.

Materialism became secondary to love.

That is what the thought of death is. Initially, it is: "Oh, my God, I'm going to die. This is it…!"

Then, in a flash, we ponder what that would mean. And, it generally goes like this: we realise that it is the things on which you cannot really put a value that matter. All the things that had been taken for granted become richer. Today, that is a common theme in conversation, in Christchurch. Small things in our lives have gained more significance.

We found we had lost most of the places in which we gathered for communion. What did we all miss? We missed our cafes, restaurants, and churches, all the places where we met for fellowship. Previously, they had been taken for granted. But after the earthquakes, people could not even find coffee. When coffee was available somewhere, it appeared that the whole town was there.

Having fresh water is something to treasure because we have had to do without it. Likewise, being able to have a shower or flush a toilet, or flick a light switch and have power come on. We have paid a huge price to appreciate what most New Zealanders consider basic amenities.

We learnt that, even as ordinary citizens, we had power within us to change others' lives, simply by acts of kindness. We saw people deriving joy from giving to others without expecting anything in return. People in areas that escaped lightly from the earthquakes and still had water connected to their homes drove across town to the eastern suburbs to knock on a stranger's door and offer to do their laundry.

I will never forget the acts of generosity and kindness that I witnessed from unexpected quarters. If they have not changed our community for the better, nothing will.

I believe the earthquakes have brought us much closer together. Not only have the earthquakes made our spirit more powerful, they have moulded it into an unstoppable force.

Again, we need only look to the Second World War generation to identify its impact. That generation had a great sense of purpose and achieved a huge amount. In their day, the country, by and large, had a single, simple view. Perhaps it was not a vision that would sit easily today, but there was clarity of purpose and a sense of togetherness which built this country through that period. They built the power schemes, the roads, housing and did a superb job laying a foundation for our nation.

They also had a much stronger sense of community that has grown out of the hardships of rationing, loss and trauma. Each community comprised of groups to enhance individuals and accommodate aspirations.

We see the same thing here. What a remarkable, psychological moment: 4:35am, 4 September 2010: 500,000 people hit by such a huge earthquake that many of us thought that we would die at that moment. Aftershocks have provided similar recurring experiences. They are unique. Psychologically, the earthquakes have united us in a manner rarely experienced in New Zealand. It is reflected in our young people and our sports teams. Look at their capacity to delve that much deeper than opponents. Cantabrians have long had that grit. As a result of suffering, it is now even more firmly harnessed within us.

This attitude was obvious soon after we had set up in the Art Gallery on 22 February. We were overwhelmed with offers of assistance. A similar outpouring had occurred after 4 September. This time, we were confident about what to expect. We instructed staff to develop a system for coordinating volunteers.

We needed to control them because many would be venturing into dangerous spaces. It was essential that we ensured their safety, knew their whereabouts, and ensured that they had appropriate equipment for the work they would undertake.

We called on the Army to assist us in managing the process. It established a register of people offering their services and co-ordinated the implements the volunteers needed. It had to be structured, because there were liabilities and accountabilities. We did not want to put people in danger and, to avoid unnecessary duplication, we needed to know where the volunteers were and what they were doing.

Initially, when students offered assistance, we were unsure

how we could use them. It took a while for us to learn about each other. We had never previously contemplated the scale of support required to accommodate the thousands of people who wanted to help.

So many people spontaneously took it upon themselves to provide help. Mark Skelton, from Glenfield, Auckland, built a truck to provide showers for people without power and water. He delivered it to Christchurch, and liaised with the Emergency Operations Centre to ensure it was efficient and useful. It was. It provided 500 showers per day.

The reaction of young people to a call for help via the social network Facebook was amazing. Ten thousand volunteers turned up within 48 hours of the quake. They swept, shoveled and barrowed thousands of tonnes of silt, caused by liquefaction. At its peak, 13,000 young people volunteered. Sam Johnson and his mates at the University of Canterbury may not have known it then, but they were creating a model of youth volunteering that has been picked up by many similar student organisations around the world. Again, it is empowerment of the community, by the community, at a grass roots level.

Every street in every suburb with liquefaction was crowded with kids with shovels, rakes and wheelbarrows, all removing silt from gardens, drains and off floors and footpaths. Young men and women, boys and girls, all determined to do their bit to restore some sort of normality. All were determined to claim back their city.

Research shows they benefited personally from their generosity. They felt a high degree of satisfaction and a new sense of community.

Hundreds of farmers came to town and formed what was dubbed the "farmy army". They arrived on trucks and tractors to help clean up the city and to distribute supplies in ravaged suburbs.

The involvement of so many strangers – students, farmers, LanSars, police, army, social workers – became one of many defining events of the earthquake: people realised they were not alone. The earthquakes motivated people to make contact.

It was not only Christchurch where volunteerism took root. Busloads of people arrived from all over the country. Some brought picks and shovels. Some brought food; others brought bedding and warm clothes to distribute to the community.

On occasions, I loaded up a Council truck with food and water to distribute to volunteers. I ran into office workers who had flown, at their own expense, from as far away as Auckland, simply to help a friend clean up his property. Many people with small earth moving machines had brought them to the worst hit areas to lend a hand.

As the aftershocks continued, people throughout the country opened their homes to Cantabrians to provide respite from the ongoing battering taking place beneath our city. People were invited to holiday on farms, spend time for free in hotels in cities; even travel to Australia and the Cook Islands for a break. All this was available for free.

People's reactions confirmed my belief that those old values of self-reliance and caring for our communities are embedded in us all. Often, we are too busy to use them. It takes an event like a disastrous earthquake to rekindle those qualities and bring people to the fore.

In response to our appeal for financial assistance, people began turning up at the Art Gallery with donations for the Mayor's Fund. Hundreds came in with $20 notes. Many only parted with their dollars in return for touching my orange jacket, or a hug. Although I was exhausted, I tried not to turn down any request. Money began arriving from around the world, in all denominations and currencies. On one day alone, we had $300,000 cash at the Art Gallery.

Sarah was tasked with recording every donor. We were determined to send everyone a personal thank you. Thousands of e-mails came in offering all sorts of assistance. We replied to as many of those as we could.

We were sent bottles of wine, which everybody was too busy to drink. At the same time, health authorities warned us not to drink water because it was contaminated. We received hundreds of knitted hats to keep people warm. Rest home residents sent us colourful patchwork quilts which well meaning residents had spent hours making. We got truck loads of blankets. People's generosity was overwhelming.

That is where the outpouring of support began – from a desire by individuals to make a difference in a time of need. It is human nature, part of our DNA. We see it all over the world. We saw it in Australia during the floods that swept through Queensland, New South Wales and Victoria only a few weeks before our disaster.

I have no doubt that it was because we all have, within us, feelings of wanting to help, civility and kindness, that we became so disgusted and angry with the looters who stole from the central city. Because the CBD was largely damaged beyond repair, it was heavily barricaded to keep people out. In stark contrast to the overwhelming feelings of compassion, a few miscreants set upon stealing from it.

Fortunately, looting never became the problem it might have. Crime actually decreased by 20 per cent after the earthquakes. There were almost 10,000 less offences committed in 2011 compared to the previous year. The decrease was reflected in all areas except sex crimes.

In the CBD Red Zone hundreds of millions of dollars of

goods, equipment and cash were available as easy pickings for thieves and looters. When the earthquake struck, everyone had run for their lives and abandoned their businesses in the Red Zone. Tills were full of money. Gold, silver, platinum, diamonds and watches were strewn about display cabinets, floors and even on the streets. With walls, doors and windows shattered, light fingers would have had no difficulty pocketing valuables.

The general manager of Ballantynes, the city's largest department store, Brian Lamont, was amazed when he returned to his store nine days after the earthquake. It had been left wide open when shop assistants and customers fled. Remarkably, nothing was stolen during the time it stood open and uninhabited.

It was not until I hunted for the Mayoral Chain in preparation of attending the Memorial Service, about four weeks after the earthquake, that we remembered it had been taken to a jeweller in the CBD for repairs and cleaning.

A link in the gold chain, which symbolically denotes a Mayor's authority, had become loose. Each link is inscribed with a name and the years a person held office. It is worn at Council meetings and public events at which the Mayor represents his local body.

I needed the chain for the Memorial Service that was to be held at Hagley Park on 18 March 2011.

On 22 February, 20 minutes before the earthquake struck, one of my staff had taken the chain to Donnell's jewellery shop in Colombo Street. Fortunately, the employee managed to return to the Civic Building unscathed.

The troublesome link commemorated the Hon. Tommy Taylor, the 29th Mayor of Christchurch. A former Member of Parliament, and founder of the New Liberal party, he died three months after being elected mayor. The link on the chain notes that he was mayor from 27 April 1911 – 27 July 1911. His funeral was the biggest Christchurch had seen.

Retrieving the chain was a risky venture. We required permission from engineers to enter the building. They accompanied the jeweller, and his wife, Jo and I into the Red Zone in a four-wheel-drive vehicle.

It was rather frightening. The possibility of being hit by falling bricks was constant as aftershocks dislodged masonry. When we got to the shop, the door would not open.

A burly USAR member forced it open with several kicks. Along with the jeweller, he squeezed inside. They found the Mayoral Chain on a workbench waiting to be fixed and cleaned, exactly as Richard Donnell, the jeweller, had left it when he fled his premises to safety.

When they picked up the chain to remove it, the loose link fell out. I have resolved not to replace that link until we have succeeded in overcoming the multitude of problems that residential Christchurch faces. Every time I put the chain on, the missing link serves to remind me that that job is still far from finished. I look forward to the day I can replace it.

The jeweller's wife, Helen, presented us with a bouquet of flowers, a speck of beauty amongst the rubble in the Red Zone.

We brought the chain back to the safety of my office. I wore it at the Memorial Service on 18 March 2011. Nobody appeared to notice the black hole where Mr. Taylor's link should have been.

Only those who have lived through the 11,000 aftershocks that had rocked Christchurch at the time of writing can understand the psychological strain Cantabrians have endured. Some of the worst aftershocks have been:

2010

4 September,	7.1 magnitude
8 September,	5.1 magnitude
19 October,	5.0 magnitude
26 December,	a swarm of 32 aftershocks up to 4.9 magnitude

2011

20 January,	5.1 magnitude
22 February,	6.3 magnitude
6 June,	5.5 magnitude
13 June,	5.6 and 6.3 magnitude
21 June,	5.4 magnitude
22 July,	5.1 magnitude
23 December,	5.8 magnitude

The large aftershocks, no matter where you are, are frightening. Few of us are immune to fear. During one aftershock, the 5.6 magnitude quake on 13 June 2011, Murray Sinclair clung to a large pillar at the Art Gallery to maintain his feet. Somebody behind clung to him.

"Everybody out! Everybody out!" The order echoed through the Gallery when the violent shaking subsided.

"We are stopping work for half-an-hour. Ring home. Touch base and see what's going on with your families. If you need to go home, go home," Murray instructed.

Inside, when the first shake came, it was so violent I thought the Art Gallery could fall down. It was not a foreign feeling. I had thought it during several aftershocks since 4 September.

As I left the Gallery, another violent tremor attacked Christchurch. I watched, horrified, as the neighbouring Gallery Apartments swayed precariously. They threatened to topple. While I had experienced numerous earthquakes inside buildings, this was the first time I had witnessed one outside. It was terrifying.

I was not scared of dying. A few rational thoughts emerged, such as, if it is going to go down, I should be with my wife. Because, in that first earthquake on 4 September, when Jo was downstairs and I was upstairs, and we were both contemplating our doom, I thought: *I should be with my wife if I die. If we have gone to all this trouble to get married,* (which I had never contemplated that I would ever do again), *that's where I should be.*

We made a decision, jointly, that we would not be physically apart. With only a few exceptions, for a year or more we were never generally any more than a few metres apart.

That was a conscious choice, because life is dangerous. We have seen it lost in an instant. Each day we entered areas which, in everybody's view, were high risk. We work in high rise buildings, and we still do not know whether there is another big quake out there waiting to strike. With no apparent end to aftershocks, nobody can dismiss the possibility.

GNS Science expert Kelvin Berryman was in the Art Gallery on 13 June when the aftershock struck. When he was satisfied the aftershock had settled down, Murray assembled the team at the foot of stairs in the foyer and invited Kelvin and the controller on duty, Jane Parfitt, to reassure us that, despite the shake's intensity, there was little to worry about.

Kelvin explained that although the two quakes were severe, they were consistent with GNS predictions for aftershocks. He doubted anything worse would follow.

Warwick Isaacs, the Timaru District Council's former chief executive, and now head of the Christchurch Central Development Unit, and several other workers escaped death by inches that day.

Strategically placed throughout the city are a series of "indicator buildings", premises with sensitive measuring equipment attached to them. The data recorded in them enables us to determine the extent of damage an earthquake may have caused, and action we have to take to ensure safety.

After we evacuated the Art Gallery following the first violent shake on 13 June, we could not re-enter the Gallery until we learned the likelihood of further danger, as recorded in the "indicator buildings".

Warwick led a Civil Defence team and engineers into an indicator building in Lichfield Street about 30 minutes after the initial earthquake. They were inside when the second shake came. Unfortunately, it was even more violent than the first one.

They fled the building and reversed down Lichfield Street with masonry and debris falling around them. I will never forget seeing Warwick and other members of the team when they returned. They were pale and shaken. They had had a close encounter with death.

Indications were that the earthquakes had caused more damage to the city. Reports soon came in confirming this. The second earthquake measured magnitude 6.3, even bigger than that of 22 February which had caused so much destruction.

Because all the unstable buildings had already fallen down, and we had quarantined the Red Zone and the hill top suburbs, no lives were lost. Nearly 50 people were injured.

As reports about damage filtered into Civil Defence, it became apparent we might have to remain at the Art Gallery all night. Jo rushed back to the apartment to gather clothes and cell chargers. It was the first time we had been separated since making our vow to remain together. It seemed a long time ago, that morning in September when this nightmare began.

2011 had been an exhausting year for everyone in the quake zone. The conversation from around November onwards in our organisation and across the city was about anticipation of a good Christmas break. Jo and I were heading to Taupo to spend Christmas with her family.

We arrived at the family holiday bach on the afternoon of December 23. I sat down in the sun to relax. I recall telling Jo how much I was looking forward to a couple of weeks with no early starts, no phone calls, and actually doing nothing other than lazing about with her. I promised I would catch a decent sized trout for lunch on Christmas Day.

Then the phone rang. It was Cr Aaron Keown. There had been a very big shake, possibly as big as the June quake, in the city a few seconds earlier. Aaron and his family had been setting out on their own holiday break when the violent shaking occurred. Now, he was heading back home.

I called the Civil Defence team immediately. They informed me the shake was potentially a magnitude six and centred east of the city.

I rang Sarah in my office and told her that I would return immediately. Because no commercial planes were flying from Taupo that afternoon, I requested she find out what else was available.

I told Jo I was returning to Christchurch but that she should stay and await her family's arrival. Goodness knows she needed the break. She agreed.

Sarah contacted Government House and then rang back that the Royal New Zealand Air Force would help. They would have a twin engine plane on the ground in Taupo within the hour.

While I fielded calls from the media, Jo drove me to the Taupo Airport. I talked with the Deputy Mayor who was already working with our communications team to set up media briefings.

I arrived at Christchurch early evening. Sarah and Cr Barry Corbett met the plane and assisted the ground crew by manning the paddles and guiding the aircraft to its parking spot, much to the apparent amusement of the Air Force pilots.

As we drove into the city, Sarah produced a pizza takaway. It looked a little worse for wear and a significant portion had already been consumed. Barry had the contented look of a bear that had just consumed a pot of honey.

They briefed me on the latest information as we drove to Council's temporary accommodation in a central city warehouse. Within a few minutes of arriving, I was fully briefed, dealing with media enquiries and on TV with Gerry Brownlee. So much for the Christmas break.

Most of us in Christchurch had relished that Christmas holiday as a time to relax with family and find respite from what had been a year from hell. That quake crushed the collective spirit of our city. Plans were thrown into disarray,

Our own teams of workers, and those of our contractors, put in extraordinary hours to patch up the city.

Many had been at a BBQ arranged to thank them for the 'above the call of duty' work they had put in. When the quake hit they put down their beers, turned off the gas barbeques, and immediately switched back into emergency mode. How they found the energy, I'll never know. They were the work-booted heroes of the city on that and following days.

Again, we had liquefaction, broken pipes, busted streets, power outages and more damaged buildings. Fortunately, there were no reports of serious injury.

I told the media that we were pulling out all of the stops; we were working to have water back on, streets cleared enough for traffic to pass, power restored and infrastructure, such as bridges, checked for Christmas Day. We were determined to give everyone the best Christmas we could in the circumstances.

The next day, I went out into the east of the city which again was the hardest hit area. Liquefaction had bubbled out of the ground again. It was heartbreaking seeing their homes. Christmas decorations told how they had tried to inject joy into their wretched lives. Beneath the decorations, mud caked floors. Outside, gardens that had been preened ready for a family Christmas were covered with silt. Streets were more munted than ever.

By Christmas Eve, most of the problems were patched up enough to give crews, staff and, most importantly, the people in our City a Christmas Day with the basic essentials.

On Christmas Day I flew back to Taupo, got out on the lake with Jo and her parents John and Marg, and caught a trout.

I was glad to be there. It had felt strange being in Christchurch on my own without Jo for a couple of days. It was the longest we had been apart for ages.

It is impossible for those outside Christchurch to comprehend how hard it has been living in the city because nothing similar has occurred in our country in living memory. When asked what it has been like, I urge people to:

Imagine the sadness attached to losing most of your town's heritage buildings and icons.

Imagine living in a town where you have lost most of your sports, recreational and leisure amenities.

Imagine living in a town without your favourite drinking places, coffee shops, restaurants and theatres.

Imagine being unable to shop or conduct business in your town's main streets.

Imagine getting lost in your town because roads are closed or lead to nowhere, and most familiar landmarks have gone.

Imagine most of the familiar buildings in your town being demolished to become empty spaces inhabited only by weeds.

Imagine your town's skyline changing character each day until it is unrecognisable.

Imagine being prohibited from entering the centre of your town because it is too dangerous.

Imagine being shut out of your business and unable to retrieve computers, equipment, records or stock.

Imagine having to walk away from a business you have built, or worked at, over generations.

Imagine not knowing where you will live in a few months time.

Imagine having to leave a house in which you raised your family and thought you would spend the rest of your life.

Imagine not knowing whether you will receive enough money to buy a comparable house.

Imagine your house being so badly damaged it is barely habitable; you do not know when it will be repaired, and you have nowhere else to live.

Imagine passing, daily, sites at which people recently lost their lives; some of whom you knew.

Imagine, daily, passing through suburb upon suburb of derelict, deserted houses.

Imagine, daily, driving at night in dark streets of houses that are unlit because they have been abandoned.

Imagine, daily, driving on streets that are dirty and broken.

Imagine driving in street after uneven street of road works.

Imagine all this happening during a bombardment that has continued relentlessly for 24 months.

Imagine waking in the night with a start as the earth rumbles and shakes your home like a toy.

Imagine lying in bed wondering whether this time you will die.

Imagine being at work; or in a shop, a cafe or a restaurant when a loud crack splinters the air. It coincides with an abrupt jolt that feels violent enough to move the earth off its axis.

Imagine holding your breath and, again, wondering if, right now, you might die.

Imagine bureaucrats and insurers holding your future in their "in" trays while your life ticks by.

Imagine the joy of discovering you have endured all this and you are still alive.

Imagine.

We have not had to imagine any of this. It is our reality. It has been since 4 September 2010.

Immediately following the 22 February earthquake, about 70,000 people are believed to have fled Christchurch. Most have returned. The only reliable data available for population movements is school enrolments, which show that at the beginning of 2012, 5000 students had not returned to school. That figure indicates the numbers who left the city permanently may be much smaller than claimed.

Incredibly, 207 of our 215 schools were damaged. About 10,000 homes in the eastern suburbs have been issued red stickers, indicating they are un-safe for habitation. Almost 1800 businesses will be demolished for the same reason.

Iconic Christchurch Cathedral, which dominated our skyline for 131 years, is being demolished. So are at least 250 other historic buildings, including another Christchurch icon, the art deco Edmonds baking powder factory (circa 1922) at Woolston, whose motto was "Sure to Rise". Unfortunately, that was wishful thinking as far as that building and many others are concerned.

Lyttelton, which nestles on the sides of towering hills beside the port that is so vital to our region, was a quaint town full of history. Many of the buildings adorning its streets and lanes were built by hard labour gangs over a century ago. The New Zealand Historic Places Trust regarded Lyttelton as one of the largest historic areas in the country. Sadly, much of the quaintness that inspired that unique place in our cultural heritage has now gone, torn down by earthquakes.

When Mr Key and I flew to Lyttelton on 23 February to assess the extent of damage, what we saw in the historic port town was alarming. Almost all the buildings on the main street had collapsed. Fortunately, the navy was there helping to provide meals and other assistance, including an emergency medical centre.

The ship's crew recounted that the frigate "Canterbury" almost rang like a bell when the earthquake's shock wave struck her hull with the force of an enormous hammer.

Having once been Mayor of Lyttelton, I felt very sad to see the town in such a state. My old flat, which had been in the Time Ball Station, had its walls blown out.

We were optimistic about saving the Station until it was completely destroyed by another earthquake on 13 June 2011.

Obviously Christchurch, previously a city comprising enchanting Victorian buildings, will have a much different character in the future. Most of those buildings were constructed by our forefathers to remind them of "home" – Britain – and they were damaged beyond repair. So were many of the next generation of buildings, dating from the 1950s to the 1970s.

After the 4 September earthquake, an energetic and vociferous group of campaigners fought for the repair of most damaged icons. Unfortunately, destruction from the 22 February earthquake was even more extensive. Buildings which may have previously been salvageable were irreparably damaged. We have lost so much history, so much that made our city unique, and so much that is irreplaceable.

It was not only iconic homes for culture and worship that were felled. We also lost the AMI Stadium, which was home to the Crusaders rugby team and Canterbury cricket, and the popular QE11 Park and Recreation Centre.

Damage to AMI Stadium meant we had to cancel hosting any of the seven games scheduled to be played there during the 2011 Rugby World Cup.

I was determined that matches should go ahead because they would have lifted morale and stimulated the economy. I made this clear to John Key early in March after he texted me the following: "Heads up. Prince William coming to Memorial service. Announcing at midday."

I responded: "Thanks. Appreciate the heads up… John, losing the RWC would be a big blow for Chch. Many businesses will be counting on a boost. Is there anything that I could say or do to help with the IRB?"

I do not doubt the Prime Minister saw the benefits that would accrue from Christchurch hosting the fixtures. Each game was expected to attract over 30,000 fans. Local businesses, hard hit by the earthquakes, saw the events as a lifeline.

On reflection, with continuing aftershocks, the appalling condition of AMI Stadium, and a growing number of tourist accommodation businesses receiving red stickers, cancelling our involvement was inevitable.

I was gutted when the International Rugby Board officials visited Christchurch on 16 March 2011 to break the bad news to us. After their announcement that the games would be played elsewhere, I said a few uncharitable words, and concluded: "Well, you are all bloody wrong."

As it turned out, they were all bloody right. Our circumstances did not improve. Aftershocks continued, more red stickers had to be issued, and our winter was dismal. Many of our citizens, their homes broken and drafty, endured one of the worst snow storms in a decade in July and August 2011. With such a harsh winter on top of earthquakes and no apparent end to aftershocks, many wondered what we had done to Mother Nature to make her treat us so mercilessly.

The All Blacks tried to cheer us. They made a special visit to the city one cold Sunday in September 2011. They put smiles on fans' faces, but not on mine. Instead of the Mayor and Council hosting the event, we were not included. Instead, executives from the Canterbury Earthquake Recovery Authority (CERA) played a dominant role. I said nothing publicly, but suspected it was a sign of the strains developing from the changing democratic circumstances under which we now worked.

Players from the English and Australian teams, that were scheduled to play here during the tournament, also visited. Their presence was appreciated but it could never make up for the loss we suffered. Many small businesses suffering financially from the earthquakes' impact, had counted on the World Cup to provide renewed economic vigor. Many feared they would not survive without the crowds and cash the games would provide.

It was a tough time to be in business in Christchurch, particularly for those based downtown. Hundreds of businesses had to relocate. Any empty building on the outskirts of the city was snapped up and turned into offices. Some small businesses worked out of garages and owners even converted bedrooms into offices and factories.

Owners of businesses in the CBD became annoyed that they could not enter the Red Zone to retrieve property. Many buildings there were in an extremely dangerous state. Each aftershock threatened to bring down more masonry which could maim or kill. Because of the randomness of the earthquakes, we never knew when they would occur, nor the strength of their attack.

Business people demanded that we let them into buildings in the Red Zone to retrieve equipment. I can understand their frustrations and needs, but they were ignorant about the risk. When there is a pause between seismic events, people relax and forget that earthquakes strike without warning. People get lulled into a false sense of security. They imagine they can pop into an alleyway, dash inside a building, fossick about, retrieve their stuff, and run out again and remain safe. That is nonsense. Earthquakes are not benevolent. They strike randomly, when least expected. They place the same pressures on our bodies as they do on infrastructure, making it difficult to break free. They do not discriminate about who they maim or kill.

We certainly learned that after 4 September. I was extremely proud of the way in which Council workers had tackled the task of putting Christchurch back together again after that first earthquake. Nobody expected a second catastrophe that would be even worse.

After 22 February, the scale of the damage was overwhelming.

But when I look now at what has been achieved rebuilding infrastructure, I feel extremely proud to be part of this Council. Although the work is essential, it is also largely invisible. People see the empty spaces where buildings once stood, and the munted houses in which people still live, and think that nothing is being done, or that putting things back together again happens too slowly.

The reality is that that is not the case. About 1000km of roads were damaged – that is almost equivalent to the distance from Wellington to the Bay of Islands. Thirty bridges were ruined. Six hundred retaining walls collapsed. The bill for repairs was estimated at $750 million, which we thought was astronomical.

Now the total bill is over $30 billion.

Consider what the Council has achieved: Not only have we temporarily reconnected the city to all of its essential services, we have embarked on a massive rebuild. To date, we have laid nearly 40km of sewer mains. Five significant new water supplies have been established with more on the drawing boards. Twenty seven kilometres of water mains were replaced within 18 months.

Twenty thousand individual road repair jobs had been carried out in the same period. Over 21,000 tonnes of asphalt laid along with over 200,000 tonnes of metal. More than 500,000 tonnes of silt, caused by liquefaction, had been removed from parks and reserves.

People forget that infrastructure belongs to the community. It is not the Council's. Our task is to look after the community's assets on their behalf. Unfortunately, on my watch, we lost a lot of it. My responsibility is to get it working again.

The resilience of Cantabrians astounds me. Few people could survive the conditions we endure without being affected psychologically. This was also felt by those who came to help and inspire us during our dark days. One such visitor, Prince William, was sent by his grandmother, Her Majesty the Queen, to represent her at the Memorial Service on 18 March 2011.

Jo and I, unsure what to expect, met him at the airport. During the journey into town I briefed him about the progress of recovery operations.

On my wrist I had red and black bands – Bands 4 Hope – that were part of a fund raising campaign and signified the solidarity of Cantabrians. I gave them to him and he wore them with pride.

I explained that we had developed a word to describe our

situation: *Munted.* At the Emergency Operations Centre at the Art Gallery, he skillfully dropped the word *munted* into conversation on a couple of occasions.

When we pulled into the Art Gallery he immediately noticed the large portable toilet block that was emblazoned with the words *Royal Flush.* A group of workers stood in front of it pointing at the words to capture his attention.

I explained that they were toilets. He immediately got the joke.

Personally, I have not yet dealt with my emotions. My trick was to suppress them by immersing myself in work. By keeping busy, I avoided confronting issues within myself caused by the traumas we have endured. Thousands of other people forced themselves to pack their emotions away during the earthquakes. While it was necessary at the time, it is not healthy and many of us are paying a price today.

While others in the team occasionally hid from view and wept after witnessing sights and hearing stories from earthquake survivors, I forced myself to retain composure. I suffered the same personal trauma as everyone else, but people would not benefit from seeing me breaking down.

My job during the earthquakes was to lift people's spirits. I could not achieve that if I revealed my own frailties. The truth was, I could not allow myself to have emotion; I cast my feelings into a pit deep inside myself. There they lay, hidden, throughout the whole ordeal.

The façade did not preclude me from experiencing the same pain, joy and sorrow felt by others. I simply could not allow myself the luxury of wallowing there. There were many times when, had I let my guard slip, I could have broken down and wept; at times, it was very difficult not to.

I consider myself extremely fortunate. Total strangers showered me with so much support when, out in the suburbs, they came up to me, and hugged me and touched me as if, somehow, it made things better for them. I do not understand it. They continue to do it, even to this day. On the hard days it has been a great reviver to my flagging spirits.

Just the other day someone came up and said: "I hid under a table with my kids for a week or two – that's where we lived. What we waited for every day, to know that everything was okay, was your voice. The sound of your voice, the way you spoke, and what you said, helped so much.

"We thought: 'Well, if Bob's there, and Bob's saying we are doing this and we are doing that, we'll be okay'."

I find it incredible. There is not a more powerful or beautiful thing that people could attribute to you.

The number of people wanting to join my Facebook site has overwhelmed me. There were thousands. Membership had reached the 5000 limit more than a year ago.

Again, when they joined, they said something really beautiful. As is to be expected in a political job, occasionally, some were critical. I have not had to worry about them because my Facebook friends take care of it. I am very grateful.

In some aspects, the mayoralty is an isolating position. Jo and I have expended a lot of emotion during this whole process. When a little comes back, it keeps you going. Daily, people still thank me for being there during the earthquake. It just blows me away.

I genuinely respond: "Thank you for being here for me."

I doubt they appreciate how important they are to me and how they lift my spirits and keep me motivated, particularly in view of some of the criticisms I have encountered since the earthquakes. People's gratitude is humbling. It is the greatest gift anyone can give me.

It has not been easy for Jo. She has difficulty accepting that she must share me with the public. She felt threatened by the outpourings of love and my capacity to return those emotions to complete strangers. It is fortunate we have built a strong, confident relationship.

Being a partner of a public figure is a difficult role. It is particularly onerous seeing that the person you love has an emotional meaning to other people. Often, that person can be busy when you need him. A partner can feel quite isolated and alone. I know Jo feels there are always a lot of people between her and I. She looks forward to a day when we can spend more time alone together.

Obviously, my emotions had to eventually boil over. It happened at the Memorial Service at Hagley Park on 18 March 2011. We were at the George Hotel waiting to walk across to the podium. The significance of the event suddenly struck me. All that we had lost, flooded in my mind. All the destruction, fear, hardships and deprivation overwhelmed me. For the first time, my guard slipped and I felt very emotional.

I managed to hold myself together as, before Prince William, the Governor General, Jerry Mateparae; the Prime Minister, John Key; Australian Prime Minister, Gillian Gillard and other dignitaries, I spoke to a crowd of 100,000. I had not prepared a speech. I talked from my heart; it just poured out of me as I said:

> *Who among us can even begin to comprehend the rhythms of life and death that have swept across our city. Who in these families gathered with us today, can truly understand why this thing has happened, and why it has happened here.*
>
> *And in the shattered homes in the worst affected areas of our city, have had to go through this terrible time not*

just once, but twice. We have to look at the uncertainty, to deal with the fear, to worry about our families, worry about our jobs, worry about our future. Why did it have to be here?

Those are answers that are very hard to give. Those are the pressures that are very hard to understand.

And how do we go forward as a city and carry on our shoulders the weight of what has happened here? How do we find a way to make sense of this thing?

And, it seems to me, that I look to the families of those we have lost, and I recognise that among those families are not just people from this city, but people who come from other nations. Whose children came here to study. Whose children became our children, and whose story is, whose lives are, now forever entwined in this place.

And there were those who came here to visit, to enjoy this place that we love – our home – the quality of life that we are so proud of – and they too became victims of this earthquake.

And as a city we have to find a way to take this quake, and we have to find inspiration to go forward as part of our processes, of just, not only grief, but of finding hope and finding a way forward.

And it seems to me that those lives that have been lost have to be given a real meaning in the city as it goes forward.

There were teachers who died in the earthquake, and I believe we have to dedicate ourselves, in this city, to building a city that honours the principles of our founders, principles of knowledge and greater learning. That way, the loss of those teachers can be given meaning. We can deliver the dream that they held for our young people and those young people who came from other places.

And, of those young students who died, we have to remember their dream. Their dream was to have a door opened into life, to gain knowledge. We have to remember that, from this, we have to give real meaning to that.

We have to make in the city a stage, a doorway through which our young, and the young from other nations who came here, can aspire to the best.

And we think of the business people who died and, of course, we think of their families. And we think of the dreams that they had and the difficulties and challenges it takes to run a business.

And these small businesses that are at the heart of the city's prosperity have suffered, and we've lost people.

So we have to dedicate ourselves, as a city, to say in this city we will rebuild in ways in which our businesses can prosper, in which jobs can be recreated.

We have to remember the linkages to all these nations: Japan, China, Korea, Israel, Turkey, the United States, Canada and other countries. Australia. As well as our own people that have been lost.

And we have to find a way to create, when the time is right, a memorial that is suitable. So that those names will walk with all of us into the future.

But in the end, it seems to me, that to give meaning to this terrible event, we have to have faith in ourselves. Not just because we need to honour those among us who have been lost. Because we have to remember that we have to hand the things that were given to us, to our children, and their children, and their children beyond that.

From suffering and pain, what we have to do as a city

is to reach into our hearts, and our spirits, and our self belief, and build the safest city, so this thing can never happen again. To build a city based on strength and optimism, and know that we will rise from this time. We will rebuild the shattered suburban fabric.

We will stand by people, and we will have a city in the future that again will be the most beautiful place on earth that you and I could ever wish to inhabit.

That is our goal. That is how we remember those we have lost. Our hearts are with them. God bless you all.

When it was over, and I sat down, I felt emotionally drained. I think it occurred because it was the first time in weeks that we had slowed down. Back over at the George Hotel, I found a quiet place and wept. It all poured out of me. I was not alone, many other people who worked in those grim circumstances did too. I have felt emotional many times since then.

Really, I still haven't dealt with my emotions today. That is true for a lot of people in Christchurch. I guess we will, in time.

It has been interesting. As a city, we went through a phase poignant for its love, generosity and tolerance; a time when we selflessly sought to help others. Having passed through that, we seem to realise issues of our own that had to be dealt with. People lost patience.

We went through a period when much of the population appeared to suffer road rage. This was not surprising, considering the state of our streets, and the number of cones and barriers motorists had to avoid as they drove over bumps and potholes. It was enough to annoy a saint. Then the EQC and other organizations, including the Council, bore the brunt of people's wrath, which was born from the frustration of delays they perceived as poor decisions and poor communications.

Next, it was people, perhaps a staff member, exploding over small stuff for no reason.

People's patience was severely tested. We had so much in our lives to deal with. We had a bureaucracy that was suddenly called on to service a situation with which it could not cope. It was a bureaucracy which people found complicated their lives, rather than helped them, and made matters even more difficult by providing conflicting information.

On top of all that, the aftershocks continued. People were overwhelmed by a sense of helplessness and a feeling that the world had forgotten them and their plight. Understandably, frustration set in.

Today, Cantabrians live in a different time scale. People have endured thousands of very scary aftershocks. On numerous occasions, we thought we would die. That fear creates a new appreciation of time. It makes every minute extraordinarily precious. Therefore, every minute spent on a phone waiting for some faceless bureaucrat to give an instruction or help solve a problem, generates anger.

That rage is born from the frustration and sense of loss that we are all facing.

So many things create within us a sense of powerlessness. Perhaps it is when we lose a building; or we notice a hill has changed its character because of slips and rock slides; or a rock that, because of its permanence, we used as a landmark, has fallen -- suddenly our world is different. We are consumed by a sense of powerlessness and feel our lives are unmanageable.

Various government departments did not help, confusing us by not controlling the dozens of conflicting messages that circulated after 4 September.

Services set up specifically to help with trauma counselling did a brisk business with people in need of psychological help.

Trauma manifested itself in many ways.

We saw this during a recent visit by Cook Islands Prime Minister Henry Puna. After the earthquake he had generously invited us to send people who needed a break to relax in the Cooks on free holidays.

During his visit here, we arranged a function at the Council to acknowledge Cook Islanders' generosity. Families who had holidayed there attended. I went around the room and asked each to tell Mr Puna what the holiday had meant to them.

"It was the first time my children had slept soundly through-out the night in eight months," the first woman to speak revealed. She wept as she recounted the experience.

"My little son, we had not seen him smile for a long time," another mother said as she fought back tears.

And so it went. More and more emotion flowed and people started breaking down as they expressed their gratitude.

That sort of reaction is not unfamiliar to us. People have been through a very hard time.

The pattern of behaviour witnessed in Christchurch after the major earthquakes conformed with the Kubler-Ross model of grief. (A lecturer at the University of Chicago medical School, Elisabeth Kubler-Ross suggested people pass through five distinct phases when confronting a life-threatening or life altering event).

There is no doubt, in my mind, that Christchurch is certainly going through them. It could well dwell here for several years.

The first phase involves denial – "this can't be happening to me!" Sometimes people are trapped in this phase which manifests itself in an inability to accept the reality of a situation.

The second phase involves anger – "how can this happen to me?" These people can be quite irrational and difficult to deal with.

Next is bargaining – "I am too old to leave my house. Surely,

I can stay here?"

This can be followed by depression. It is a sign that a person has accepted the inevitability of their situation, but is not yet ready to surrender.

Finally, there is acceptance. It is time to move on.

From left: Mayor Bob Parker, Minister of Civil Defence John Carter, Prime Minister John Key and Minister for Earthquake Recovery Gerry Brownlee at a press conference.

Photo: David Wethey

The damaged iconic Cathedral without its spire. The billboard in the foreground promotes the Rugby World Cup and AMI Stadium. No Rugby World Cup games were played in Christchurch.

Photo: Jamie Ball

Lyttelton's historic Time Ball Station. Bob Parker had once lived there.

Bob Parker retrieving the Mayoral chains from Donnell Jewellers'
shop in the Red Zone. They were delivered for repair minutes before
the 22 February earthquake.

Photo: Jo Nicholls-Parker

A car crushed by rubble from the iconic Anglican Cathedral.

Photo: Jo Nicholls-Parker

Earthquakes devastated the historic town of Lyttelton.

Falling masonry crushed cars.

Christchurch treasured the historic Canterbury Provincial Council Buildings (built 1858-65). The Council is determined to rebuild them.

Photo: Jamie Ball

Surburban streets turned into lakes of mud and silt as liquefaction
bubbled out of the ground.

Farmers from around the South Island flocked to Christchurch
to lend a hand to shift tonnes of silt thrown up by liquefaction.

Photo: Jamie Ball

Bob Parker (orange jacket, centre) at a press conference. Eventually 1200 journalists from around the world covered the catastrophe.

Photo: Jo Nicholls-Parker

Bob Parker playing guitar at the Band Together concert at Hagley Park on 23 October 2011. Playing with him are Paul Kean and Alan Starrett.

Thousands of students spontaneously responded to a Facebook
cry for help to remove liquefaction from suburban streets.

Children quickly adapted to their broken environment. Bob Parker ad-
vocates rebuilding the city to reflect their needs, not those of the past.

PART THREE

LOSS OF THE Anglican Cathedral, around which the city was built in the second half of the 19th century, symbolizes more starkly than anything else, the magnitude of the catastrophe that has befallen Christchurch. Nothing was more iconic; not just to Cantabrians, but to thousands of people throughout New Zealand and around the world. The Cathedral was a major tourist attraction. The Cathedral was a symbol of our strength, our heritage and our aspirations.

Therefore, it is not a surprise that its demolition has caused a furor. Thousands have participated in demonstrations calling for the work to stop. They have even called upon Queen Elizabeth II to intervene. She summoned John Key to a private audience immediately after her Diamond Jubilee celebrations in June and asked him to explain the situation.

Earthquake damage was not new to the Cathedral. Bits and pieces had fallen from it in other earthquakes over the years. But this time it was much worse. It suffered superficial damage in the 4 September 2010 quake and even more in an aftershock several months later on 26 December.

Unfortunately, the 22 February 2011 earthquake was too much for it. The spire came down, a large gable was badly damaged, and part of a roof collapsed. Engineers found colossal pillars supporting the structure had weakened. More masonry fell from the Cathedral during subsequent aftershocks.

Initial reports that 20 bodies lay buried under the Cathedral's rubble proved wrong. Fortunately, although tourists were seen in and around the building before the earthquake, nobody was injured or killed.

The last straw for the old Cathedral and many other seriously damaged heritage buildings was the quake that struck on 13 June 2011. The entire western end of the Cathedral, including the mighty Rose window, crashed to the ground and the building suffered huge structural weakening.

The Anglican Bishop of Christchurch, Victoria Matthews, announced the Cathedral's deconstruction on 2 March 2012. She pledged that a new Cathedral would rise in the Square, and cited cost and safety as reasons for pulling it down. The decision brought upon the gentle, pious lady odium I previously considered reserved only for Mayors.

In the meantime, until a new permanent Cathedral rises in the Square, its temporary replacement has potential to become a tourist attraction in its own right. Designed by Japanese architect Shigeru Ban, it will be made from cardboard.

My understanding is that even though the Cathedral is being pulled down block by block, it could still be rebuilt. However, I am not of a view that it should be.

Restoring the Cathedral, exactly as it was, is not being honest about what transpired here. Obviously, the city has changed dramatically since the Cathedral's cornerstone was laid on 16 December 1864. It was already changing before the tragic events of 22 February 2011.

Christchurch's establishment believes strongly that the Cathedral should be put back the way it was. That is understandable. Their forefathers had a large part in building it. However, today we live in a new world and a new time. The world in which we grew up is gone forever.

There is no disputing that the Cathedral site is sacred. It is undoubtedly spiritual. It has become iconic. We must consider whether putting the Cathedral back together again, exactly as it was, but safer, is the best use of an iconic image.

Why not, instead, seize upon our loss as a unique opportunity to combine the visionary aspects of architecture, spirituality and history to make a bold statement? Let us create an image so powerful that it makes people pause to reflect and pray. Let us build a new icon that captures our heritage, our pain and loss, and demonstrates our resilience and our aspirations for the future.

In my view, the icon would be much more powerful if it was able to portray what has happened here, while at the same time point to where we are going.

Therefore, the counter argument that I am finding increasingly attractive is that we should retain part of the Cathedral's ruins and incorporate them into a modern structure. I would like to see the base of the steeple kept as the stump to which it was reduced when its spire crumpled. That image, I believe, is really symbolic. I would like to see as much of the walls kept as possible. Obviously, we should strengthen those areas to make them really safe.

We could then enshrine the original building's ruins in a glass case. The remains of the Cathedral, perhaps the west end, with the most sacred part – the sanctuary, which contained the altar – could be entombed within that glass case. Perhaps, because it is so holy, it could be enclosed with the roof and walls.

There could be many parts of the old Cathedral incorporated into the design, particularly the floor; it is a very beautiful tiled floor, similar to one you would find in a Roman ruin.

I propose precious artifacts such as stain glass windows and other religious icons should be salvaged and, when a new edifice is built, they should be suspended within an invisible structure.

Within the new building, we should be able to identify the shape of what was once there, although most of it would be preserved as ruins.

The other end of the space would morph into a huge spire, twice as high as the old one. Being that size would make it inspirational, a symbol of our aspirations for our city and our people.

When I grew up, the Cathedral spire was the tallest feature in the city. It was a beacon. I would like it to be that again.

People who lost their lives in the earthquake died on a beautiful, warm day. Why not keep the temperature inside the space at the same temperature it was at 12:51pm on 22 February 2011? Why not make the atmosphere inside similar to an Eternal Spring?

Such a bold vision would catapult us into the 21st century and demonstrate that our generation refused to cower before nature's whims. She knocked us down, but we got up to rebuild and live again.

I would like the message contained within a new Cathedral to reflect: who and what we were; the story of what happened; and, through the steeple, where we are going. It can be inspirational, even more inspirational than it was before.

At this stage, only one thing is certain. That is, due to its nature, its position, and the people charged with the task of replacing the Cathedral, it will be sacred.

The debate about what should rise from the rubble in Cathedral Square encapsulates much about where we stand today as a people. Christchurch's establishment is determined we should recreate the past. More progressive thinking envisions us not reconnecting solely to what we were; it sees us breaking free from the shackles of the past and picking up the cudgels of the future.

I tend to support the latter view. We have a rich history of which we are justly proud. Whatever rises on that sacred land must be more than a monument to the past. It must be a clarion for the future.

A major shift has occurred in all aspects of the city's being. It is a change which is not exclusive to Christchurch. It is occurring throughout New Zealand. The cultural, and consequently the spiritual, mix is changing at a rapid pace. New Zealand, including Christchurch, which has long been the most English city in the Southern Hemisphere, will be completely different in 30 years time.

It is a truism that some good can emerge from bad experiences. Often, it is simply lessons about how to avoid repeating our mistakes. One of the blessings to emerge from our recent disasters is that we are forced to confront urban renewal issues we struggled with for years.

What we were born into in Christchurch was a 19th century vision of the way the world was, and should be. What we have an opportunity to create now is a city worthy of the 21st century.

It presents a challenge rarely imposed upon a generation. We are tasked not only with replacing the city's main icon, the Cathedral, but with replacing much of the city itself. Undoubtedly, the transition must pay cognizance to our history. Conversely, our planning must accommodate future demographics, technologies and the like. It is an extraordinary challenge. While it is very exciting, it is also extremely daunting.

Unfortunately, elements of a vociferous battle to halt demolition of the Cathedral have been anything but Christian. Bishop Matthews has been subject to vile and disgusting abuse from individuals involved with the campaign to save the Cathedral.

She has been treated extremely badly. If Christchurch has become a city in which the public will attempt to destroy a person with an opposing view to their's, I do not want to be part of that society.

I support her views on rebuilding the Cathedral. Now is the moment in our history where we have to rewrite our future. The Cathedral represents old ways and old power structures. Of course we should lovingly remember that part of our history and retain part of the Cathedral to honour that. But we must also look to the future.

The Cathedral's interior is beautiful. The outside is just a big old grey building. The challenge is: do we shake off the shackles of the past, or show the world something new, different, and with more aspiration?

Before the earthquakes, parts of the city were decaying. Over time, we had lost many of the traditional industries that were based there. Manufacturing had gone. Foundries had gone. Many buildings were empty and fewer people visited areas that in previous generations had thrived.

Council had spent considerable time investigating various strategies for rejuvenating areas that were failing. It was a slow and often controversial process. Change usually is.

Many people accepted that dramatic changes were necessary to rejuvenate Cathedral Square and surrounding business areas. Over the years attempts had been made to do it, but none had succeeded.

My vision, when I became Mayor, was to make Christchurch a city that lived and breathed and responded to the world in which we now live.

That was why one of my goals, in the first mayoral term, was to acquire land and motivate some great design and vibrant conversation about the direction in which we should head. It was rather controversial and met considerable resistance.

That vision led us to purchasing the so-called Henderson properties. The decision caused much debate and was misread as looking after a developer who was on the brink of bankruptcy.

It was nothing of the sort. It was an attempt to acquire land to protect a vision the Council had for that part of the city. As it turns out today, we are fortunate to have those properties in our land bank. They provide an opportunity for the Council to exert considerable influence over the city's reconstruction.

The Greater Christchurch Urban Development Strategy, which I chaired, created a master plan for the city and surrounding areas. It recommended redeveloping the CBD by incorporating significant residential capacity within it.

As a result of the plan, considerable work had been undertaken prior to the earthquakes to determine the needs and character necessary for transforming Christchurch into a modern city.

From three years of consultation, and 3250 submissions, we learnt residents' views on the sort of place they wanted Christchurch to be in the future. Many people considered the city's urban fabric would be enriched by having more of them living within the CBD.

They felt an inner city urban population would enable the central city to grow and prosper. With people inhabiting the place, a whole new retail pattern would arise. Cafes, restaurants, theatres, markets and services catering for a stable inner city population would abound, thereby rejuvenating the area and producing a vibrancy to bring people back to its streets.

Timing of the work proved fortuitous. With three quarters of the central city damaged in the earthquakes, we felt confident we knew residents' desires about the shape and character of a future city. Our planning placed us ahead of the game and enabled us to respond quickly to the city's needs.

Within days of the earthquake, Mr Marryatt began working with central government to plan how the city would operate during its recovery. While the city was still under a State of

Emergency, they discussed the city's reconstruction and the type of government agency required to make it possible.

His objective was to protect the city's sovereignty by ensuring Christchurch continued to be run by the City Council, rather than from Wellington. He spent considerable time clarifying roles and responsibilities between the Council and Government.

Although Government said we should proceed, I was disappointed. I detected Government officials had little confidence that the Council could mastermind the rebuild.

The business community's view was no better. A prevailing attitude was that the Council might be able to construct a footpath; it doubted that it could plan a city.

It incenses me. Our staff is very talented and passionate about the city. The time, effort and dedication to keep the city going during and after the earthquakes is not generally appreciated.

At the time of the February earthquake, 6000 businesses, employing 51,000 people, operated in the central city. To continue trading after the earthquake, most businesses relocated to suburbs. Many now question whether the central city area is worth saving. They doubt whether firms will return to the CBD and whether it is safe from future seismic activity.

It will, in fact, be the world's safest city. Throughout Christchurch, rigorous investigations have been undertaken into soil structures to set standards to protect our buildings against the worst that Mother Nature might throw at us.

New Zealand is not alone in having its significant cities straddling earthquake zones. Many of the world's mega-cities are built on fault lines. These places gave birth to towns because they are located in rich areas. They often had minerals under crusts that had been smashed and broken by seismic activity. They had mountains thrust up by collisions between tectonic plates. They provided resources for the future because from the mountains flowed water for harnessing power to drive industry. Generations have considered that advantages from living with these threats outweighed the dangers.

Most of the world's cities are near rivers or the sea, which means they could be prone to liquefaction during a catastrophic earthquake. Would the world's great cities fold up and flee adversity similar to that which we have experienced? Of course not. They would rebuild and confront the future with optimism, just as we will.

I am in no doubt that Christchurch must be rebuilt. Seismic safety can be achieved; it is dependent upon the technologies deployed when rebuilding the central city. To enable this to happen, we have in place the most stringent safety standards in the world.

Having obtained a green light from the Government to prepare the central city plan, the Council embarked on a novel approach. We invited citizens to provide their ideas for the city's future. We called the project *Share an Idea*.

We had no preconceived ideas about the outcome. The only parameters we set were that the city's grid street pattern should remain because the town's most important inheritance is its layout. It is ancient and special, and it would be foolish to abandon it.

Designed by Edward Jollie in 1850, the street grid is a vital part of the city's character. It is the envy of many other New Zealand cities. It provides good, efficient access to all parts of the city, and beyond.

It also contains extensive infrastructure vital for rebuilding. Utilising it will enable us to reconstruct the city without incurring overwhelming costs associated with laying new sewer pipes, water mains, electricity, phone lines and data streams.

We launched *Share an Idea* at a Community Expo in May 2011. People had six weeks to present their ideas. Although still contending with aftershocks and living in broken homes, they turned out in their thousands to have their say.

A *Share an Idea* website received more than 58,000 visits during the six weeks it operated. The Community Expo, which ran for two days, attracted 10,000 visitors who shared their ideas on post-it notes, by making a video, answering questionnaires, or building their central city out of Lego.

YouTube, the media, e-newsletters, and a 160,000 household letterbox drop were also used to stimulate public involvement.

Designers and architects provided inspiration through a 48-hour Design Challenge, which we held at Lincoln University.

Fifteen teams took part in the Challenge, with seven people in each, including engineers, planners, urban designers, architects and landscape architects.

We brought international experts to Christchurch to explain how other cities recovered from disaster: Manchester, following an Irish Republican Army bombing in 1996; San Francisco following the 1989 earthquake; and Victoria, Australia, following the devastating 2009 bush fires.

Sir Richard Leese, who oversaw the regeneration of Manchester, urged Christchurch to have vision, leadership and courage when considering its city for the future. A significant risk was that without courage, Christchurch could be rebuilt on the image of its past.

He suggested consideration should be given about the type of icons the city would construct.

"You have an opportunity, don't waste it," he urged.

Charles Eadie, who led the recovery of the central business district following San Francisco's earthquake warned that one of the biggest obstacles to a successful reconstruction was people's reluctance to accept change. That resistance was evident from the public, politicians and business people.

Douglas Ahlers, of Harvard University, commended us for developing a central city plan, but warned that that was the easy part. Implementing it would be difficult. He urged Christchurch should have one vision, and speak with one united voice.

We were overwhelmed. Citizens provided us with 106,000 ideas about the type of place we should turn central Christchurch into. Nobody can deny the people have spoken on this issue. They went out of their way to do so. Heaven help us if we ignore their suggestions.

What sort of city centre do they want? To sum up, in a nutshell, they want the central city to be one that is green, safe, compact, accessible, and fun to live in.

They want the Avon River to be more of a focal point, rather than hidden away as it currently is. They want a friendlier, more vibrant and greener Cathedral Square. They called for 500 new green-rated buildings, gardens and parks.

They want buildings to be low rise, seismically safe, sustainable, good looking, with strengthened heritage buildings.

They want the CBD to be more compact; they want to redevelop the Convention Centre; they want ultra-fast broadband, free Wi-Fi, free car parking and bus routes.

They want the central city to be a great place to live and work with public art and performing arts venues and playgrounds.

They want it to be easy to get around, with walking and cycling paths, and a network of tree-lined streets. They want a city for people, rather than cars.

Christchurch has long been known as the Garden City. I have suggested that best description of the place envisaged by the public is a *City within a Garden*.

Prior to the earthquakes, we had consulted the world's best urban thinkers about developing the central city. We were astounded that through *Share an Idea*, people told us they wanted exactly what the experts had recommended. It was a massive public endorsement of the direction we had considered best for Christchurch.

Parts of the business community were appalled. One property owner described the public vision as a "rubbish pipedream". He claimed the Council's approach terrified many developers and would scare investors away.

A 200 strong group with property interests described the plan as a "vision of Utopia with little attempt to take economic realities into account".

They demanded that the plan should change because if it did not work for business, it would not work at all.

Obviously, we have conflicting sector views on how to rebuild an area which people fled in their thousands. Most say they will not return to high rise buildings. Who can blame them? We saw them trapped when fire escape stairwells collapsed. We saw ordinary office workers, men and women, abseiling down the side of buildings to save their lives. We saw that scores of ordinary workers were killed in buildings we assumed to be safe. Getting people to return to where all that had happened could be extremely difficult.

I have told the business community that the people of Christchurch presented them with a gift. They told them what it will take to attract them back into the central city. Instead of fighting public opinion, the business community needs to accept it for what it is. It should embrace public opinion and make people's ideas work.

They need to remember we are rebuilding the city, not for us, but for our children and grandchildren. It must relate to the world they will inhabit, not the world we grew up in, because that world has gone forever.

That is why on Memorial Day I gave my speech the way I did.

When I thought of the people who had passed away, I thought about the young people. They were all looking for a future. They were all here picking up skills that would prepare them for the future. The older people who died, the tourists, they were here because they wanted to enjoy something that was unusual and had a quality of life. And, the old people in our own community, they wanted a place in which they could afford to live out their lives with dignity. They paid the ultimate price by being in the city on that day, at that time. We have a responsibility to them to create a place to fulfill their dreams for the future. We also owe it to future generations.

We asked the community for their opinions and, what was really inspiring for us was that they came back and said they too supported the type of urban development that we thought was really important.

We are not surprised about the amount of pressure being exerted on the Council for reconstruction to be undertaken another way. We expected it. But we cannot ignore 106,000 suggestions from members of our community. Lo behold any politician that does.

As part of our research, we looked at the economic yield from all the floor area in the city. We found that there were a few high-rise buildings that sucked up all of the investment and the need for office space. The tallest buildings were those that had been built during the property boom of the late 1980s.

When we analysed buildings' economic performances, we found they had seldom made any real income. The only way those buildings were successful economically, was through inflation, when land and capital values rose. In terms of return on the original investment, they still charged the same rents they had charged in 1986 or 1987, when they were built. Those buildings have not really been economic.

Many of the buildings were owned by syndicates comprising people who live outside Christchurch. They are not property developers or investors; they are people whose accountants suggested they should buy into a partnership in a building which the accountants were buying.

They were invited to invest perhaps $100,000 each, along with maybe 20 others. The real profit has usually been gathered from the eventual sale of the building.

Economically, tall buildings did not stack up.

I'm very keen that we develop a strong strategy around rail. We have a great rail system around the city, but we do not use it to capacity. There is no doubt in my mind that, when you look at forecasts, we need rail for the future.

The long-term growth projections for Christchurch show that 30 years out, 70 per cent of our roads will be gridlocked at peak times, compared to perhaps seven per cent today.

The only alternative to fixing that, apart from developing a rail system, is to double the size of roads, which does not really solve traffic problems. It is also costly. Think about the cost involved in buying all the land needed for roads, including the cost of shifting all the houses and shops that are there at the moment. It is far more costly than using the opportunity we now have to develop an efficient rail system.

We need innovation and creativity in the city. It is the young creative people who drive cities. There is no doubt in my mind that when the University of Canterbury moved out to Ilam in the 1970s, the city began to decay. It sucked the vibrancy and life from the city that universities bring. That is a loss from which we never recovered. If we re-established tertiary education in the central city, we would bring 20,000 young people into the heart of the city every day. Creative young people make cities function.

I am keen for a new sustainable, architecturally brilliant

university campus to rise in the centre of the city. I would love to achieve that, but I am not getting too far with it at this stage. However, some foreign investors have expressed an interest in the possibility and I remain optimistic.

Obviously, the central city has to be a place where people want to do business. Bringing people and ideas back into its heart will bring business too.

If we are going to attract people back into the central city, we need to be very innovative, after what happened there. My belief is that once people come into the middle of the city, and they can walk and cycle places very easily, and enjoy quality living, they will not want to return to living in suburbia.

A developer will tell you the success of a new subdivision depends on the first properties sold. Therefore, they go to immense trouble to satisfy their first clients. They will not let just anybody build the first house in a new urban development. They want their first residents to exude quality, thereby doing their marketing for them.

Often, developers will want to meet those clients personally; they may even want to build a house for them. They will be looking for a good example of the quality of life their development will offer.

To us, there is only one way to establish the central city as a haven for living. That is to reinvest in our own treasures immediately – the stadium, the Convention Centre all of those significant amenities that we lost. And, that is what we are doing.

Share an Idea has been hailed as an astounding success, not only in New Zealand, but around the world. In November 2011 it won the Co-creation Award. The Netherlands-based awards recognise the most original and successful co-creation initiatives. It is the first time the award has been made for an initiative outside Europe.

Share an Idea was nominated by Capgemini Consulting, a global business employing 120,000 people, after they read about the initiative on a Dutch news website. *Share an Idea* was one of 49 projects nominated for the award. Judges said the *Share an Idea* initiative "stood out from the others".

Chairman of the jury, Jaco van Zijll Langhout, said: "*Share an Idea* is an inspiring example of co-creation, which established co-creation with their community in several ways and at several moments in time: an online platform to post ideas, a Community Expo, workshops and road shows, to develop the city centre together.

"The response on this initiative was overwhelming: more than 106,000 ideas have been shared and more than 10,000 people visited the Expo. Next to developing the new city centre, the result of this co-creation is also a stronger community."

The 4 September earthquake made Gerry Brownlee the most powerful man in New Zealand. In some ways, he enjoys even more power than the Prime Minister, John Key.

In a single day Parliament unanimously passed the Canterbury Earthquake Response and Recovery Act 2010 which placed unprecedented power for running the City in the hands of the Minister for Canterbury Earthquake Recovery. Currently, that responsibility falls on Mr Brownlee's shoulders.

Those powers were due to expire on 1 April 2012. But after the 22 February earthquake, it was replaced with the Canterbury Earthquake Recovery Act which extended those powers.

While the power provided by the new Act has received some scrutiny from academics and legal experts, most of whom have expressed reservations about dangers it poses for democracy, it generated surprisingly little debate.

In effect, the Canterbury Earthquake Recovery Act has stripped all the mayors and councillors in Christchurch, and the neighbouring councils of Selwyn and Waimakariri of their authority in regard to rebuilding their damaged areas. Nothing can be done without the approval of Mr Brownlee or the Canterbury Earthquake Recovery Authority (CERA), the Government department created specifically for the purpose of rebuilding Christchurch and surrounding areas.

I understand why the government adopted this form of control for rebuilding Canterbury. It is essential reconstruction progresses swiftly so that normality is restored as quickly as possible to enable us to contribute to the country's economy.

When announcing the creation of CERA, the Prime Minister, Mr Key, explained the organisation would support Mr Brownlee in getting the job of rebuilding Christchurch done.

Mr Key pledged that rebuilding Christchurch, and surrounding areas, was one of the Government's highest priorities. He believed the task was too large to be completed by the region's existing authorities.

It would involve billions of dollars of taxpayers' money.

"The job requires a significantly more centralised response – but one that works alongside the Christchurch City Council, other councils and local government agencies, and also provides ways for the community to have input," Mr Key said.

Because of the unprecedented sweeping powers the Canterbury Earthquake Recovery Act contains, I do not believe it has received the scrutiny it warrants.

The explanatory note introducing the Bill said it was founded on the need for community participation in decision-making processes, while balancing this against the need for a timely and coordinated recovery process.

"It is necessary to put in place stronger governance and leadership arrangements for the rebuilding and recovery of greater Christchurch from the cumulative effects of the 4 September 2010 and 22 February 2011 earthquakes.

"In developing the bill … the following factors were taken on board:

- the scale of the post-earthquake rebuilding effort. Recognising that the 22 February earthquake represents an incomparable natural disaster in New Zealand's history;
- lessons learnt from international experience and from the recovery planning after the 4 September earthquake, including the strong indication to have a single entity in charge of, and responsible for, the recovery efforts;
- the need for timely and effective decision-making powers; and
- the significant coordination needed between local and central government, residents of greater Christchurch, Te Runganga o Ngai Tahu, NGOs, business interests and the private sector," it said.

"This Bill recognises that current institutions simply do not have the capability to deal with a disaster of this magnitude.

"Institutional arrangements with specific powers and access to streamlined regulatory processes are needed to meet the challenges of recovery."

The Bill made provision for public input into reconstruction through consultation processes and community forums.

"This ensures, local people will have the ability to express what's important to them in developing and carrying out the plans for rebuilding Canterbury," it said.

"Planning for the recovery of the greater Christchurch region will occur through the development of a long–term recovery strategy which will be developed by CERA in consultation with

Christchurch City Council, Environment Canterbury, Selwyn District Council, Waimakariri District Council, Te Ruanga o Ngai Tahu, and other parties deemed necessary," it added.

The Bill provided for a mandatory recovery plan for the CBD to be produced by CERA within nine months of the bill being passed.

CERA, a new Public Service department, was established by way of an Act of Parliament on 29 March 2011 to coordinate the recovery effort under the leadership of its chief executive. Roger Sutton, previously Chief Executive of Orion, the Council's power company, was subsequently appointed to the position.

"Christchurch City Council will lead development of the CBD recovery plan (including community engagement), with input from CERA, Te Runanga of Ngai Tahu, and Environment Canterbury.

"It is expected that Christchurch City Council will develop a consultation plan to engage the many views from within the Christchurch communities," it said.

Because of the urgency required to restore Christchurch to a city that can pursue its economic destiny, the legislation gives the Minister extensive powers to overcome obstacles which could inhibit recovery.

The Minister has carte blanche in regard to doing virtually anything on private and public land. He can restrict or prohibit a person's access to any building in Christchurch. If necessary, he can acquire land; place Council plans and policies in abeyance; order demolition of homes and buildings; and close roads.

CERA's chief executive, Mr Sutton, is tasked with developing a recovery strategy for Christchurch, in consultation with councils and Ngai Tahu, but it must be approved by Mr Brownlee.

If the Minister is not happy with plans, he is able to change them in any way he wishes.

The Minister of Earthquake Recovery is also vested with the authority to circumvent the Resource Management Act, if he considers it will impede the reconstruction process. Soon after the bill was passed, Orders in Council were introduced to streamline resource consent applications in Christchurch.

It is not solely the Resource Management Act that the Minister can usurp. There could be more than 23 other Acts, including the Building Act, the Conservation Act, Local Government Act, Reserves Act and Transport Management Act. Some say those powers could well apply to all existing legislation. It is little wonder that constitutional lawyers and academics have expressed concern about the extent of the Minister's broad and unprecedented powers.

While some might see these powers as draconian, I doubt they contain any malice and are considered to be genuinely needed to re-establish Christchurch's viability as quickly as practicable.

CERA's Chief Executive has authority to control contracts councils enter into, and he must be consulted before his counterparts within councils complete any contract. If they do not involve CERA, a contract can be declared null and void.

CERA's Chief Executive is also empowered to instruct staff to break into any properties they deem necessary to complete their functions under the Act. They can also remove personal effects and fixtures and fittings. They have power to order a building to be demolished.

They can demolish buildings without obtaining the usual consents. If they decide to close roads, there is no right of appeal and there is no right of objection to a notice of intention to take land.

The Act denies a right of appeal against decisions by the Minister and Chief Executive. In some circumstances issues can be referred to the High Court or the Court of Appeal.

The extent of the Chief Executive's sweeping powers is obvious in clause 76, which reads:

"Power of chief executive to order compliance.

"(1) If any person has not complied with any lawful direction given under this Act, the chief executive, may, for the purpose of enforcing compliance with or preventing any further non-compliance with the direction, make a compliance order requiring that person –

(a) to do any specified thing; or

(b) to cease any specified activity.

(2) a compliance order may be made on the terms and conditions that the chief executive thinks fit, including the provision of security or the entry into a bond for performance."

Government will keep its control over the city for at least five years.

Government will use Orders in Council to maintain the rebuilding programme's momentum. The process will involve the Minister submitting proposed regulations for Cabinet approval. They will be signed by the Governor General at a meeting of the Executive Council. This represents a significant departure from the established convention that the Crown could not legislate without Parliament. It is actually government by decree, rather than governing through established legislative processes.

A group of 27 legal scholars, from all six New Zealand law faculties, concerned about the unprecedented powers the Act gives the Minister, called for it to be reconsidered. They are concerned it sets a dangerous precedent and lacks traditional safeguards.

"We share New Zealand's deep concern about the physical damage to Canterbury and the personal trauma this has caused the region's residents. All levels of government have an obligation to help the people of Canterbury rebuild their homes, businesses and lives as quickly as possible.

"However, while we are united in wishing to help Canterbury recover, there is a risk that the desire to do 'everything we can' in the short term, will blind us to the long-term harms of our actions. In particular, abandoning established constitutional values and principles in order to remove any inconvenient legal roadblock is a dangerous and misguided step.

"Yet this is what our Parliament has done in one day, by unanimously passing the Canterbury Earthquake Response and Recovery Act 2010. It represents an extraordinary broad transfer of law making power away from Parliament and to the executive branch, with minimal constraints on how that power may be used. In particular:

- individual government ministers, through 'Orders in Council', may change virtually every part of New Zealand's statute book in order to achieve very broadly defined ends, thereby effectively handing to the executive branch Parliament's power to make the law;
- the legislation forbids courts from examining the reason a Minister has for thinking an Order in Council is needed, as well as the process followed in reaching that decision;
- Orders in Council are deemed to have full legislative force, such that they prevail over any inconsistent Parliamentary enactment;
- persons acting under the authority of an Order in Council have protection from legal liability, with no right to compensation should their actions cause harm to another person.

"These matters are not simply 'academic' or 'theoretical' in nature. Over and over again, history demonstrates that unconstrained power is subject to misuse, and that even well intentioned measures can result in unintended consequences if there are not clear, formal measures of oversight applied to them.

"We do acknowledge that the powers granted by the Act have some restrictions on their use. They only can be used to achieve the objectives of the legislation (although this is very broadly defined). Five key constitutional statutes are exempted from the ambit. Orders in Council inconsistent with the New Zealand Bill of Rights Act 1990 may not be made. Parliament can review and reject Orders in Council, albeit through a rather slow and protracted process.

"Nevertheless, the vast amount of law making power given to Ministers, renders these limits insufficient. In particular, there needs to be tight restrictions on the enactment a Minister may change through an Order in Council and clear and precise grounds that justify any such change. These grounds also need to be open to view by the judiciary, to ensure that they really are met in any particular case.

"Any claim that such safeguards are unnecessary because the Act's powers will be wisely and sparingly applied, and the informal 'consultation' and 'public pressure' will ensure that this happens, must be resisted. Only formal, legal means of accountability, ultimately enforceable through the courts, are constitutionally acceptable.

"Furthermore, the Act now stands as a dangerous precedent for future 'emergency' situations. This earthquake, devastating though it has been, will not be the last natural disaster to strike New Zealand. When the next event does occur, inevitably, there will be calls for a similar legislative response, which will be very difficult to resist, given this example.

"Finally, we emphasize that we have no partisan agendas to pursue here. The fact is that all MPs of every party joined in the action. They did so with the best of intentions, driven by an understandable desire to display their solidarity with Canterbury's people.

"But we feel that action was a mistake, and they too quickly and readily abandoned basic constitutional principles in the name of expediency. We hope that with a period to reflect on their actions and the consequences they might have that they now will revisit this issue in a more appropriate manner," the statement concluded.

A group of lawyers appointed by the Council of the Auckland District Law Society Inc. to consider public issues also aired concerns over legislation introduced to deal with the 4 September 2010 earthquake. Their concerns are equally as valid.

"The Canterbury Earthquake Response and Recovery Act 2010 gives unparalleled powers to the Crown," their statement began. "This article reviews concerns regarding the appropriateness of such powers being handed over by Parliament to the Crown.

"The Canterbury earthquake was a destructive event unmatched in recent New Zealand history. Christchurch, and the greater Canterbury region, will take several years to fully recover from the devastation wrecked by the earthquake," it said.

"Special legislation was passed by Parliament after the 1931 (Napier) earthquake, providing specific measures to address particular problems caused by the Napier earthquake. In response to the earthquake, and earlier labour strikes, Parliament also passed the Public Safety Conservation Act in 1932, granting the government more general regulation-making powers which could be used in future emergencies," the statement recalled.

"The Public Safety Conservation Act 1932, was inspired by the emergency laws passed during the First World War. The 1932 Act did not grant general legislation making powers to the government, but only the power to use emergency regulations. The Public Safety Conservation Act, as amended, required that regulations passed under the Act had to be referred to Parliament for subsequent review and endorsement. It also required Parliament to meet within 28 days of the Act being invoked. The legislation was limited in its scope to emergency situations, and regulations were of limited duration, to be passed solely for the purpose of 'the conservation of public safety and order and to securing the essentials of life to the community'."

The report said Parliament responded to the 4 September earthquake with a much wider and more general emergency legislative measure, even though it was a less destructive earthquake with less local impact than the Napier quake. (On that point I think I would have to disagree with them).

"Effectively, the government may repeal or amend any legislation, at will. Furthermore, this would be done without any parliamentary monitoring and only a very limited right of review," it said.

The legislation does not restrict itself to excluding Parliamentary review, it also prohibits judicial review.

"This is despite the powers contained in the Act extending well beyond making emergency regulations, to amending 'any New Zealand statute'.

"Quite uniquely, the Act limits judicial review, and potential attempts to question the appropriateness of any ministerial action … The powers granted to ministers under the section effectively amount to an unfettered right to legislate by decree.

"The powers under the Act permit the Crown to arbitrarily make exceptions from compliance with existing legislation. Possible examples could include exempting law enforcement agencies from the Crimes Act 1961 … or excluding all heritage buildings in a region (or nationally) from the protection of the Historic Places Act.

"The power to modify acts of Parliament could be used to increase the rate of GST or income tax, without reference to

Parliament.

"The ability to extend (sic) the provision of any New Zealand statute could be used to extend the application of the new Search and Surveillance Act to even more government agencies.

"Regulations under the Public Safety Conservation Act 1932, were intended to be passed only during periods of national or local emergency, and had to be referred to Parliament for subsequent approval," the statement said.

The Canterbury Earthquake Recovery Act has no such limitations.

"It has long been an established constitutional principle that the Crown could not legislate without Parliament. Parliamentary sovereignty has been at the cornerstone of our constitutional arrangements since at least the 17th century," the statement said.

"Parliament has effectively authorised the Crown to amend any legislation, for any purpose. These purposes need only remotely relate to the earthquake."

The statement maintains it was questionable for Parliament to transfer such extensive powers to the Crown, thereby abdicating its own responsibility on behalf of people.

"Specific legislative changes may well have been required as a result of the Canterbury earthquake (although that is by no means certain), but these could have been implemented as and when needed, by specific legislation. This would have been a much more appropriate response to the challenges of the earthquake," it said.

As Mayor, the person elected by more than 68,000 people to lead Christchurch, the Canterbury Earthquake Recovery Act makes me, and every other councillor in the region, politically impotent.

The reality is that Mr Brownlee, as Minister of Earthquake Recovery, is in charge of the entire city, with much more power than any Mayor would ever have. The next most powerful person is the chief executive of CERA, Roger Sutton.

I believe a better approach would have been to strengthen the Council with services now contained within CERA. By doing that they would have demonstrated respect for the Council, the community and structures that already existed. After all, the local authority has been duly elected.

The government's strategy was to set up their own system and tell everyone else what to do.

Had they approached the Council and explained the issues and objectives, we would have built an organisation to deliver a magnificent result. We had many of the skills, and much of the information, necessary to achieve this within our existing structure, anyway. As it has turned out, they have had to rely heavily on us for this.

By creating a new department, the Government displayed a lack of confidence in our ability. This was unfounded. We have a huge array of professionally skilled people within our organisation, all of whom are making significant contributions to rebuilding Christchurch. This was evidenced by the extent to which the central city plan we submitted to government was largely adopted as the way the city should move forward.

The Christchurch City Council instigated, and carried out, much of the planning work that will result in rebuilding the central city. It also has responsibility for rebuilding the wider city's infrastructure.

The CERA model has resulted in a significant amount of duplication. One of CERA's primary roles is to provide plans for rebuilding the city. This is a task at which the Council excels. Yet, we have seen CERA embark upon planning projects which were already available from the Council. One was an economic development plan. They employed people to achieve a result that was, in my view, only a slight rewrite of projections we had already completed.

Not only does this duplication cost money, it also slows down the rebuild.

CERA has built a 'dream team' of bureaucrats who have to prove themselves. Unfortunately, some of them are constantly trying to reinvent the wheel. Local government is a huge, complex business. CERA's people are new to it and do not understand its complexities, which are massive. While they have theoretical knowledge, they do not have the skills, resources or contacts available from within the City Council. As a result, they are dependent on us and our systems. That creates friction between our organisations.

CERA has grown like Topsy. Originally, it was going to comprise of a staff of 60 people. Now staff numbers have topped 200.

Despite tensions which exist from time to time, the system appears to be working reasonably well, now that it is embedded. Because it houses people from a whole spectrum of government departments, ranging from social services to physical services, we deal with only one organisation – CERA – and problems get resolved much more efficiently. Previously, after 4 September, we had to deal with each Government department individually.

After the September earthquake, Government established the Canterbury Earthquake Recovery Commission (CERC) to oversee the reconstruction of the city. I sat on the body with Mayors from Selwyn and Waimakariri and two Commissioners appointed by Government.

It turned out to be little more than a two way filter with information coming from the Government to the region and then reporting back to Government again. It was a slow and diffused leadership model. Clearly, a better structure was needed.

I am told the Government cast around the world for a solution. It decided on creating a new Government department, locating it at the centre of the disaster, and placing other relevant bureaucracies within it. Hence, the birth of CERA.

Government first took control of the city on 23 February 2011 when it declared a National State of Emergency. It was a correct decision because we could not have managed without input from central Government. However, it did not come without considerable cost to central Government and the longer the emergency lasted, the more expensive it became. The State of Emergency could not continue indefinitely. When it was withdrawn, the Government felt it needed control over the recovery phase.

Work on the type of government agency required for the city's reconstruction had begun a few days after the 22 February earthquake at meetings in Wellington at which Tony Marryatt participated.

His objective was to protect the city's sovereignty by ensuring Christchurch continued to be run by the City Council, rather than from Wellington. He spent a considerable time clarifying roles and responsibilities between the Council and Government.

While agreeing to CERA being established to avoid the leadership and communications problems that eventuated after the 4 September earthquake, he insisted that the Council should be involved in rebuilding infrastructure and drafting the Central City Plan.

The only role he discarded was responsibility for demolishing damaged buildings. We were happy to concede that because the demolition could involve us in conflicts with the city plan and our ownership of a large number of buildings within the city.

While people might think we were sidelined by Government,

this obviously was not the case. Through Tony Marryatt, we have had significant influence, including input into Cabinet papers discussing the formation of CERA and the formation of the Central City Development Unit. That is not to say we have not had arguments and disagreements. Of course we have. It would be impossible to agree on everything in a project as big and complex as this.

We were also invited to provide input into the Canterbury Earthquake Response and Recovery Bill. While we considered it an incredibly invasive piece of law making, we accepted that without central Government, we would be unable to manage the scale of recovery required to rebuild the city. We accepted the CERC concept, which had led to Government departments operating independently of each other and too many people making different decisions, would not work. It had caused public confusion and frustration.

We felt affronted that the Government's initial proposals did not include the Council participating in planning the city's future. After all, this was our city, and *our* people deserved their say in shaping its future. Tony's persistence had resulted in us being included in the Bill.

The common view held by Wellington bureaucrats, the Canterbury Employers' Chamber of Commerce and, I suspect, Mr Brownlee too, was that the Council would not be able to cope with a rebuilding programme.

Tony and I discussed their proposals and agreed that he should travel to Wellington to argue our case that Cantabrians should be involved through the Council in reconstructing their shattered city.

As it turned out, public participation is our strongest restraint against abuse of power that could emanate from the Canterbury Earthquake Recovery Act. The tens of thousands of people who participated in the *Share an Idea* project morphed into a body that politicians must take seriously.

Democracy itself is the major check against abuse occurring under the Act. The Government must realise that it depends on Christchurch's support if it is to have any hope of winning the 2014 general election.

National did very well in Christchurch at the 2011 general election. The positive way the Government had responded to earthquakes undoubtedly helped. Mr Key visited Christchurch frequently, and Mr Brownlee also put in the hard yards.

The city rewarded them with their first victory in the Christchurch Central electorate since it was established in 1946. Other National Party candidates did very well. National enjoyed a massive Party Vote swing. There is no doubt that the Government would be foolish not to listen to the people of Christchurch. We saw *Share an Idea* as the vehicle for delivering their message.

Christchurch's importance to National to win the next election means the Government will have to stand by us and help solve our problems.

I just hope the Government listens intently on the matter of asset sales. We have endured considerable pressure, from Treasury in particular, to sell our publicly owned assets to fund the rebuild. Even the Prime Minister has waded into the debate. He suggested we should consider a partial sell down of assets. This is anathema to most Cantabrians. We treasure our assets and are proud that we have kept them when other councils sold theirs'.

Mr Key suggested in May 2012 that, in view of the cost of rebuilding the city, the Council should consider partial asset sales. He advocated it would be in our interests to consider a mixed ownership model similar to his proposals for the electricity sector and Air New Zealand. Under that scheme, Council would retain 51 per cent and sell down the balance. The money would be used for the rebuild.

"They have a unique position where they have got some very large profitable projects and they might want to think about the mixture of those assets," Mr Key said.

He gave an assurance the Government would not force the Council into a decision.

Mr Brownlee, too, signaled the Government would encourage asset sales.

Early in the piece, Treasury knocked on our door. I suspected they had been sitting in Wellington dying to scrutinize a major council. The earthquake presented an opportunity to burrow inside New Zealand's second largest local authority. I imagine they salivated at the prospect of investigating our holding company CCHL, Christchurch City Holdings Ltd, looking at its assets, its operations and the prospects for selling them.

Treasury projected we had a $1 billion shortfall in funding for rebuilding the city. They suggested we consider which assets we could sell to make up the difference.

We were surprised. We did not consider that we faced a funding problem. Did they not understand our normal annual budget was $650 million? This year it is $1.4 billion. Finding $1 billion would not be a problem.

The amount of money required for repairing Christchurch is not in dispute. However, the way Government wanted us to raise the money is.

I felt an appropriate approach would have been to ask us how we intended meeting our obligations, rather than telling us how to go about the funding for them.

Finding money was not difficult. We have a renewals budget through which, every year, we set aside up to $200 million for projects such as renewing pipes and streets and repairing footpaths.

We saw the rebuild as similar to our renewals programme, except it would be on a larger scale. Our fiscal responsibilities were for the amount required after we received payments from insurance and Government subsidies.

We decided the rebuild was actually about renewals that were necessary in one part of the city as a result of damage caused by the earthquake. We suggested we should take $50 million out of the budget each year, for four years (it is already allowed for in rates), and put it into recovery. We started that process in 2010.

Rolling it out over 20 years, we can fund the debt without having to sell anything. The impact on rates is two per cent.

It is really simple. It does not require Treasury to come down from Wellington to tell us to sell the Christchurch International Airport. However, if the Government determines we should sell assets, we can, in my view, be forced to under the Canterbury Earthquake Recovery Act.

Intense discussions regarding asset sales have taken place with Treasury behind the scenes. They have had the Council under a microscope. They have scrutinised every aspect of our operation. We accepted that. We are open to any suggestions that could make us more efficient.

However, there is also an ideological issue at play. As reflected in legislation currently before Parliament, the Government is intent on restricting councils' investment activities.

Most Christchurch ratepayers want to keep their strategic assets, particularly if we can fund the city's reconstruction without inflicting undue pain on them. Most of these investments – the airport, Lyttelton port, the stadium, playing fields – took many generations to build. They are investments that reflect the aspirations of those generations.

Selling them to pay for reconstruction in one hit fails to recognise that the facilities are going to be used by future generations. Borrowing is a fair method of funding because it spreads the cost over generations that will enjoy and benefit from them. This reflects the infrastructure's inter-generational values.

In 1989, when local government was reformatted, Christchurch did not sell its asset as others did. The Council of the day decided the best way ratepayers could get money back from assets they had built over decades was from dividends returned from those investments. The money would be distributed across the people of the city. That is the fairest way. That is still our approach.

However, there is continuing pressure from Treasury, to a certain extent Government, and the Canterbury Employers' Chamber of Commerce, who all advocate we should sell our assets.

We agree that we should be aware of asset values and review their community benefit. But we must also acknowledge that some assets provide significant strategic value for the city. For instance, the airport, the port and the electricity company are natural monopolies that are very important for Christchurch. They have a long-term role to play in the city. They should continue to help drive investment, exports, and the community's well-being long into the future.

Independent directors, not councillors, run those companies very competitively. They are great companies.

We also own a couple of companies that are remnants of the old days of the Council. One is City Care, a contracting company that was our old Works Department. It is doing incredibly well at the moment because it has secured a fifth of the work to rebuild Christchurch's infrastructure.

A one per cent return is about normal for a contracting company like City Care, which is really low. City Care is returning us closer to 15 per cent, perhaps even higher, at the moment.

An argument exists that because it is not strategically important to the city, City Care is something we could consider selling. We have to ask why we actually have shares in City Care, and whether it would be better to sell it and look for another form of investment that might benefit the community more.

Our investments currently return, on average, from both dividends and capital growth, about 15 per cent a year. A return of that magnitude cannot be dismissed lightly. If we sold those assets and deposited the money in a bank, we would earn only a three to 4.5 per cent return.

Because we own these companies, and they are all lowly geared, we are able to borrow money as cheaply as the government – at about four per cent interest.

My argument is why give up a 15 per cent return on your investments for a four per cent, or less, return from a bank when we can already borrow that money for considerably less than most people?

We are in a period of low interest rates and naturally rates will fluctuate over time. But like any prudent organisation, we hedge against that. We have a very smart treasury operation within Council and we employ external advisers. We manage our investments and our debt as well as any organisation in New Zealand.

I have no doubt the majority of people in Christchurch do not want us to sell Council owned assets. We always need to be pragmatic and, in the normal course of events, there may be some we might seek permission from our community to handle in a different way. At this point, we do not need to do that.

I believe that is the reason some members of Government, including Mr Brownlee, cut up a bit recently. They had said we needed to sell assets. We disputed that and explained the reasons. That flummoxed them, because they thought they would stimulate a great debate and force us to do it.

They might still try, for any number of reasons. The new sports stadium is a case in point. We proposed building an uncovered stadium that seats 35,000 people to replace AMI Stadium which was munted in the earthquake.

Government wants us to erect a stadium with a roof on it, to provide all weather protection. The benefits from doing that are obvious and most people would welcome the concept. However, we refuse to add a roof at this stage because we consider it is a bridge too far for our community as far as costs are concerned.

While, personally, I acknowledge the advantages of the stadium being covered, I cannot accept it is prudent to spend $50 million to $100 million on that right now.

I suspect the Government is going to insist on the roof and demand that we sell a portion of our assets to pay for it. The only other alternative is to find money from private commercial investors or perhaps benefactors. Given most stadiums are loss making enterprises it will require innovative thinking. However, we will leave no stone unturned in order to shape our city as the most desirable in New Zealand.

Negotiations over funding options are conducted on a friendly, low key basis between Tony Marryatt and the Central Christchurch Development Unit Chief Executive, Warwick Isaacs. Tony has to operate within the confines of our Community budget. He reports back to me and I take the issues to the Council. If the Council is not prepared to sell assets and the Government insists we do so to pay for a stadium roof, the Government may have to consider issuing an Order in Council to force a sale.

For us, politically, that is the safest option because it would be abundantly clear to citizens that we are being forced to comply with an unpopular approach. If Government does use that heavy-handed approach, it will have to bear the negative fall out it is likely to generate.

Strict guidelines govern the amount of debt a council can

carry. Council's policy precludes it from borrowing for operating expenses. It will borrow only for capital investment.

Ratepayers' contributions for paying interest on loans are confined to a maximum of eight per cent of the cash collected by rates each year. Incidentally, rates are only about one third of our budgeted income, the other two thirds of the money comes from our investments, fees and charges, and Government subsidies. Many other councils have much higher levels of rates tied up in paying debt, some up to 20 per cent. Projections indicate that even if we borrow $1 billion for the rebuild, we will retain the lowest rates in any metropolitan centre in New Zealand.

Fortunately, the Council was well insured, and the cover will provide a huge amount of money for reconstructing our infrastructure. Government, through standard subsidies, will also make a large contribution, particularly for roads. Because roads go beyond the city, as part of a national network, the Government's subsidy is about 50 per cent.

We have always been confident that by combining all our funding resources we would be able to meet the cost of the city's rebuild. I hope others now accept that, and see that we do not need to sell assets to meet our obligations.

Tough economic times that have placed constraints on Government spending are promoted as another reason for us having to sell assets. We were told the Government simply does not have sufficient revenue to fund projects. Treasury has posed questions about why someone in Auckland should have to pay for the rebuild in Christchurch through their taxes.

We dismissed this argument as nonsense. Consider the amount of GST the rebuild will generate. This alone could pay for rebuilding the city. Based on reconstruction costing $25 billion, the GST take from that is not very different from the amount required for the city's recovery – about $3 billion.

The combined earthquakes hold a dubious record. They are the world's most expensive economic disaster after the Japan tsunami. Everyone grappling with these enormous challenges is working under immense pressure. It is little wonder that nerves are often frayed. Occasionally it results in terse words and regretful behaviour.

Mr Brownlee must be under immense pressure. He has an enormous responsibility for Christchurch, not to mention his other parliamentary duties as Minister of Transport and Leader of the House of Representatives.

His style is to shoot from the hip and ask questions afterwards. This was reflected in March 2012 when he sparked a near diplomatic incident with Finland by suggesting that Finns were uneducated, unemployed and did not respect women. A few days before this outburst, he had publicly humiliated me when he described me in the media as a "clown".

At the time, I was out of the country. I felt absolutely humiliated. Over time, I have been called many things that are a lot worse than a "clown". But this was particularly galling because it is essential that the Minister and I have a close working relationship. I was concerned that if the Minister responsible for my city had lost confidence in me, I could be a barrier to the city attaining the outcome to which it aspired. I seriously considered resigning.

The incident occurred when Treasury was picking through our books looking for reasons we should sell assets, particularly the power company Orion; the Council appeared dysfunctional, and there were suggestions that Commissioners should take over. The Government did not want to appoint Commissioners.

In an interview with a journalist, I was asked what the problem would be with appointing Commissioners. I responded that there are two reasons this should not happen. The first was that

Commissioners were appointed by Government and CERA, its agency, already enjoyed sweeping powers. I gave an example that if CERA said rates needed to be 15 per cent for five years, and the Government agreed, then that would happen. Because Commissioners are appointed by the Government, nobody in the room would be contradicting the decision. They are all going to say "yes". If the Government wanted to sell the airport, they would agree with that too.

I pointed out that if councillors were in the room, they would not agree to those proposals unless there was a compelling argument. Councillors are answerable to the public, unlike Commissioners or CERA, who are responsible only to government. Effectively, if Commissioners were running Council, all those decisions could be transferred to CERA. Nothing in that statement was new. I had spoken to media along these lines on other occasions.

Prior to the interview I had had a conversation with Gerry Brownlee about a paper from Treasury which I had found quite unpalatable. In it Treasury proposed putting people inside the Council to look at our business unit which they thought they could make more efficient. They wanted to know the worth of our investments and returns from them. They also suggested we should generate more income by increasing rates significantly. Another proposal for raising money was that we could corporatise water.

We told them that if they wanted to learn about our business, they could find information in the Annual Report, which was available online. We did not mind giving Treasury the information, but to put people into our operation at that time would have disrupted budget processes that were underway. All this was going on at the time that the journalist interviewed me. Naturally, I did not discuss any of these subjects with her.

The same journalist rang Mr Brownlee that night and, I think, may have slightly misrepresented what I had said, because I had not mentioned the Treasury papers to her.

Whatever her question, Mr Brownlee hit the roof. I believe he thought I had disclosed the very things Gerry and I had discussed that morning. He thought I was making political capital out of our conversation of earlier in the day.

Had I not received an apology from Mr Brownlee, I would have resigned. My main concern about resigning was not that I felt slighted and humiliated, but that if the Minister for Earthquake Recovery who needs to have a close working relationship with the Mayor and vice versa, had lost faith in the Mayor, and genuinely thought he was a clown, then my presence would be detrimental to the city's best interests. If that were the case, then I would not be doing my job.

Before I got the chance to resign, news about Mr Brownlee's apology came through, and I had the Council urging me not to act hastily. Being overseas was not a good place from which to resign.

The first time I saw him after that incident was at the Memorial Service at Latimer Square for the first year anniversary of the earthquake. We shook hands and he profusely apologised for what he had said.

We have got too much to do together to let something like that get in the way. We have our clashes, but I do not dislike him. We've had enjoyable times together. His direct no-nonsense manner, although sometimes misdirected, in my view, has pushed all of us to perform to the limit. Arguably, it has been essential in trying to keep this massively complex recovery programme focused on moving forward. It is not an easy task. I doubt many others could do it.

At the end of July 2012 the Government released its long awaited review of Council's Central City Recovery Plan. I regard Warwick Isaacs, head of the CCDU, as a mate. He is as straight as a die and, as a former District Council Chief Executive, understands local government people and processes.

The CCDU's task was to take the draft plan that the Council had handed to the Minister on 19 December 2011, review the great community vision contained within it, determine the final location and form of the "anchor" projects, and redevelop the rules that would see the plan's effective and timely implementation.

From the moment the CERA Act was implemented the Christchurch City Council was, in essence, relegated to a sub-servient role. It was hard to see strangers from the Wellington bureaucracy take over the roles that we were elected to do.

Now, after all the work we had done with our community, we were again reminded of our relative impotence in our own city. I have no doubt that much of the so called "dysfunction" in my Council was as a result of the overwhelming sense of power-lessness we felt. In that sense, we were like every other citizen in Christchurch: powerless in the face of a massive natural disaster; powerless in the face of large bureaucracies running insurance and repairs; and unable to feel that we were being heard.

The CCDU's task, as much as we tried to rationalise it, made us feel that we were, again, being pushed to one side. The message seemed to be: "nice try guys, but now the real team is going to finish the task".

When we originally designed the plan, the area of greatest conflict for the Council had been business' concerns about the rules controlling their activities. They called the rules "draconian".

The central city had been closed behind cordons for almost two years. Business had abandoned it. Gerry Brownlee's task was to build enough confidence in the plan to encourage developers and investors to return. The plan sat on the Minister's desk for four months before he acted. It was a frustrating time in which we wondered what would happen.

Given only 100 days to review and amend our ideas, the CCDU immediately recruited specialist planners, commercial property consultants, and financial and investment specialists to tackle the task. It seconded several key Council staff.

At the Council, our hearts sank amidst rumours that the CCDU was making significant alterations to our award–winning plan. We had laboured over the strategy, incorporated 106,000 public submissions into it and spent over a week listening to the public's views and suggestions. The draft plan had consumed our lives for nine months; it was our baby. We fretted that it had fallen into the hands of people who might brutalise it.

It was not until almost 70 days into the CCDU's process that I received my first glimpse of their work. It looked promising. The Minister had remained true to his word because the plan reflected key elements contained in the community's vision.

Still included were the Otakaro-Avon river park, a serpentine green space on both sides of the river replacing roads and creating a new "water front" for the City; so were green boulevards and a compact central core of low rise buildings. A Convention Centre, bigger than we had proposed, was there. The sports stadium was also included, although it had moved to a new central location, and featured a grand covered roof. Missing were the rules which, after all, were the main reservation Mr Brownlee had voiced about our plan. He had portrayed them as unworkable and too complex.

I arranged for Councillors to receive a preview of the CCDU's thinking. It revealed that several anchor projects, such as the sports stadium, the swimming complex and the Convention Centre, had been shifted to locations different to those that we had suggested.

Timing for building some projects, such as the new central library, had been brought forward. We were dismayed that more attention was not given to residential redevelopment, but we were assured that the version prepared for Cabinet approval would give it more prominence.

Generally, councillors felt positive. However, the rules were still invisible. I was also concerned about some other aspects that remained unaddressed.

To sort things out, Warwick arranged a meeting between his key planner, Don Miskell, and my Council team which comprised Tony Marryatt, Mike Theelan, our planning chief, and I. We intended to raise awareness around issues that concerned councillors. The meeting did not go well.

I may have been a little grumpy at that meeting. I endeavoured to cajole the CCDU team to place more emphasis on urban residential development and to reconsider the location of some venues. For instance, I thought the swimming pool development should be closer to the site of the old Centennial Pool complex. This location would place it closer to the existing residential area in the central city.

We wanted more emphasis on sustainability and a "green" city. We also wanted more control over the buildings' designs. None was hinted at in the new plan. Mike Theelan had become increasingly frustrated that the plan lacked the urban vision that his team had presented to Mr Brownlee.

One of Warwick's staff began taking notes of our gripes. I demanded to know who she was.

"Is she a spy from the minister's office?" I snapped. "We're here for a frank discussion, not a report to the headmaster. I'm simply asking the questions that my Council and community will want answers to".

Some weeks later, at a business breakfast, when cooler heads prevailed, Warwick reminded me about my outburst.

"Do you remember that comment you made about one of my team?" he asked, pointing to the woman in question. Feeling slightly embarrassed I admitted that I did.

"Well," said Warwick, "do you know where she comes from?"

"No," I said.

"She's from the GCSB – the Government Communications Security Bureau. She's a bloody spook, mate! When you called her a spy, we all cracked up. That's exactly what she is."

We had a good laugh.

I guess the CCDU must have been keen on tight security. I hoped that I was not now on their files as a person who needed close watching. In any event, she was a very pleasant and professional person, but I never fully understood her role or the point of having her there. None of us were subversives.

Councillors were incredulous when we met the CCDU member responsible for writing the new rules. She was already familiar to us from the council hearings on the Draft Central City Plan. There, she had acted on behalf of business leaders who had briefed her to oppose our proposed ordinances.

"That's a poacher turned game keeper, Bob," Cr. Barry Corbett whispered to me. "What the hell is she doing here? It must be a major conflict for her."

Ironically, while earlier Gerry Brownlee had described the Council's planning rules as incomprehensible, the CCDU had gone full circle. They had largely adopted them. However, they had neglected one of the most important platforms of the community vision: that the city should be built with sustainability as its goal.

We had anticipated that, in view of the public's submissions, the CCDU would have prepared a plan that retained our focus on a design-led approach. Instead, they had placed before us a scheme that focused more on investment, and less on quality. It neglected detail about transport and roads, aspects we considered crucial when selecting sites for the big projects. It was not what our community had told us it wanted. We were not happy, and we told them so.

Later, Tony, Mike and I talked to Warwick Isaacs about our disappointment. He promised to reflect on the Council's feelings. He had a long talk with Mr Brownlee who, God bless him, also took our concerns on board.

The outcome was an agreement that they would reintroduce a design panel to vet all proposed buildings to ensure that some of the low-quality tilt slab developments that had blighted our city would not be repeated. The design panel would have to reach decisions on applications within five days – a big challenge, but essential to avoid delaying progress. All new buildings would be classed "Restricted Discretionary", which meant that to obtain consent, they would have to meet good urban design standards.

Detail about city traffic flows (including a review of the one-way streets) was missing. We were assured it would be developed following the release of the 100–Day Plan.

The city would still be low rise and green spaces would abound. It was a great compromise.

Ngai Tahu was intimately involved with the Council in forming the draft plan we presented to Gerry Brownlee. The plan emphasised the city's close relationship with its original Maori settlers.

Because we had worked together, I proposed to Mark Solomon, the Kaiwhakahaeri (leading elected figure – essentially, a similar role to my own) of Ngai Tahu, that we should stand together to protect our community's vision.

Our constituents had entrusted the plan to us. I proposed a meeting to establish whether we both thought it fulfilled its original promise.

Although it was, and should remain, a confidential discussion, we both identified areas of concern.

It became obvious that, if we were to stand together with the Minister at the plan's launch, then we still needed further amendments. We were concerned that in constructing the plan to appeal to the business community, which it certainly would, it had lost elements important to our community. As a consequence, its vision had become too focused on bricks and mortar. To be accepted by the public, both its vision and presentation needed to be humanized to reflect the goal of a city for people. A place not just for business, but where citizens would feel they belonged too.

The Council was also concerned about the plan's affordability. Mr Brownlee had publicly described our original draft plan as a 'nice wish list". Now, his plan would cost considerably more than the one we had devised. At one meeting, I congratulated Gerry Brownlee on his "wish list". He enjoyed the irony of the joke. He has a great sense of humour. I guess in his grueling role he needs it. Frankly we all do!

Warwick Isaac met with the Council to discuss the work he and Tony had undertaken with our General Manager of Corporate Services, Paul Anderson. Paul, previously a high-flyer in Telecom, was effectively our Chief Financial Officer (CFO).

His work in managing council's finances, with Tony Marryatt, through the harrowing years of the earthquakes has been widely praised. He was a finalist in the NZ Institute of Accountants public sector *CFO of the Year* in 2011.

Council agreed with their formulas for apportioning finance to management, construction and major anchor projects that would build the framework of the Central City Plan. Warwick felt confident that when the Minister presented his white paper to his Cabinet colleagues, they would agree to the mechanisms we had jointly put in place.

The plan would require $155 million more than we had originally budgeted for anchor projects. We could meet this without affecting our overall debt profile. In fact, we could save around $20 million over the next eight years.

I asked Warwick if he was confident Cabinet would accept this proposal.

"Have you got a plan B, Warwick?" I enquired.

"No," Warwick responded, "Cabinet has been kept well informed and I've had no push-back on the funding."

Provided the Government helped us with cash flow in the first couple of years by paying its share of the projects first, which Warwick was confident it would, there would be no additional impact on ratepayers. It was very do-able. Councillors supported this.

I had delayed agreeing to write an introduction for the CCDU plan until that moment. I did not want to endorse a plan until I believed that we could deliver it, and that it met our community's expectations of a new, safe, sustainable and low rise city designed for people.

I met with Mark Solomon to establish whether we were united on our approach and that we could stand beside the Government. We agreed that we had the changes we wanted. Mark's team had been pressuring the CCDU to go back to the Council's Draft Plan format. This placed emphasis on the people's vision, and drew strongly on the Ngai Tahu story.

I left the meeting elated. Mark and I parted with a handshake and a hongi. From our perspective, it appeared everything was in order for the plan's launch. I agreed that its unveiling should take place in the foyer of Council's main building Te Hononga, the place of coming together.

Five days before the launch, Gerry Brownlee summoned the Council to a meeting at the historic Canterbury Club, on the banks of the Avon river. No staff was to be present. Expecting to learn that Cabinet had approved the final plan and its funding model, we were excited. However, a shock awaited us.

At the meeting, Mr Brownlee outlined funding mechanisms for the key anchor projects that were to be delivered jointly by the Council and the Government. Despite the agreement we believed was in place with Warwick Isaacs, Cabinet had rejected our preferred joint funding model.

In essence, there was now a funding gap of $1 billion that Council would have to find. Councillors were shocked. A number, who had supported the CCDU plan and Mr Brownlee's role in it, expressed dismay.

Cr Barry Corbett spoke for most of us. He told Mr Brownlee how disappointed he felt; he could not now support the plan. I watched the Minister closely as Barry delivered a powerful speech. Mr Brownlee appeared shocked. I also expressed my concerns to him.

"We've worked in good faith alongside you, despite numerous barbs from yourself and others, Minister. We've been put under enormous pressure, had our roles largely usurped by CERA. Many of my councillors are suffering from great personal stress, but have stayed the course, and now we get delivered this message? God knows, we want to support you next Monday (the launch day for the Central City Plan) but this is a real blow.

We're speechless," I said.

Depressed, shocked, angry and disappointed, we trudged back to Council headquarters. I invited the councillors to debrief in my lounge. The conversation reflected our mood. We agreed to meet the following afternoon to discuss a way forward.

As we departed, I noticed lights still burned in the CCDU offices. I hoped, for the sake of the City, that they knew about the Council's reaction and were toiling to solve the problems.

Early next morning, Sarah Owen informed me: "The Minister wants to meet Council urgently. Can we do it at nine this morning?"

We looked at the committee meetings and hearings that councillors were already committed to. We settled on a meeting as late as possible.

We waited in my lounge for Mr Brownlee and his team. Warwick turned up first. I felt for him. He had negotiated with us in good faith, believing Mr Brownlee would fully accept our joint funding proposal. He had been very confident. Now, he had to face us knowing that the rug had been pulled out from under him.

Mr Brownlee and his team bustled into the room. In his usual no nonsense way, he cut straight to the chase.

"I got the impression you guys left the room feeling unhappy last night. I think it's because I didn't explain the new funding model well enough, so I'm going to take you through it again," he announced.

He explained the Government was confident that we would jointly find private equity partners to pick up some of the capital costs, that the large land purchases Government had decided to make in the city – which would devour much of the budget we had expected the Government to put toward the capital building programme – would also lead to land sales and, thus income flow further down the process.

Mr Brownlee introduced several innovative ideas, and gradually our mood shifted. We could see that the funding gap could close, that the total gap would be considerably less than the $1 billion, and that ultimately, if the extra "aspirational" element of CCDU estimates could not be met, we could fall back on the Council's original budgeted costs for the project.

The plan's launch was going to be bigger than Ben-Hur. The Government team took over the whole main foyer of our new Civic Building. A three dimensional computer model of the city spread over six large television monitors. It provided an immersive experience that allowed guests to soar over and around the proposed new city centre.

A hard copy book of the plan was in short supply. Its design was elaborate. It mimicked the Draft Plan the Council had handed to the Minister six months earlier.

A huge number of guests attended. The world acclaimed Cathedral Choir sang on the stairs, a jazz band stood by ready to play, the bar groaned under orange juice and bottles of wine. We were ready to go.

The Prime Minister swept into the room, media swarmed around him, and Mr Brownlee paced about like an expectant father. I placed the gold chains of office around my neck and sought out Mark Solomon and his team. We hongied and greeted the young kapahaka group.

"Its all about them, my friend," Mark said, pointing towards the youths.

The launch was a stunning success. The audience listened attentively as first John Key, then Gerry Brownlee, followed by myself and Mark Solomon, spoke. The audience waited politely, anticipating the unveiling of the plan which comprised the giant screen video presentation. The announcement was precisely timed to coincide with the day's main television news shows – 6pm.

The audience was stunned. They soared over computer generated images of the city we envisaged rising from the rubble and empty lots caused by the devastating earthquakes we had endured.

The video ended. Silence. Then spontaneous applause started. Long, sustained, enthusiastic applause. Gerry beamed. I caught the Prime Minister's eye; he smiled and nodded in my direction. I shook Mr Key's hand and walked over to Mr Brownlee and Mark Solomon. The crowd's positive reaction swept away any doubts we may have had about the plan's merits.

Over the next 24 hours, the positive response was overwhelming. Early polls indicated that more than 70 per cent of people loved the plan. Most of the business community was ecstatic, although some knew their properties would be purchased by the Government for major projects.

The implementation of the plan will present us all with challenges, from ensuring quality of design to funding the great aspirational projects. But I am confident we can fulfill the vision. Yes, we need to be innovative, to work harder and faster than ever before at a consenting level and to change our planning rules from complex and demanding to friendly and enabling. The opportunity is truly exciting. The challenge is worth taking on; the future is worth fighting for.

I recalled my words at the Memorial Service in Hagley Park, just weeks after the terrible loss of life in the 22 February quake:

> *From suffering and pain, what we have to do as a city is to reach into our hearts, and our spirits, and our self belief, and build the safest city, so this thing can never happen again. To build a city based on strength and optimism, and know that we will rise from this time.*

We will rebuild the shattered suburban fabric.

We will stand by people, and we will have a city in the future that again will be the most beautiful place on earth that you and I could ever wish to inhabit.

That is our goal. That is how we remember those we have lost.

I have no doubt now that we can do that. We will rise up, we can have our city again. And it will be great.

Seismic events similar to those that physically ripped apart Christchurch rippled around the Council table as well. Little did I realise, when I cast my eye over councillors attending that first meeting in 2010 that, before long, the Council would be so dysfunctional I would have to call on Government for help to resolve the problems within it.

Controversial issues, inexperience and personalities around the Council table created events that, occurring in the wake of a disaster the Prime Minister had described as New Zealand's "darkest days", were intolerable.

Much of our city lay in tatters. Thousands of our people endured unprecedented hardships. Aftershocks continuously battered our morale. If ever there was a time in New Zealand's history when we needed to rise above petty political issues and self interest, this, surely, was it. Unfortunately, it did not happen.

Because of the pressures the earthquake placed on the Council to get the city back on its feet, much of the support we should have provided councillors was overlooked as we concentrated on projects considered more important. On reflection, this was a mistake.

New councillors were thrown into the roles without proper induction or training. Several had little experience and were ignorant about the traditions and principles of local body politics. There were factions within the new group, which I should have identified and dealt with.

The Council's executive team of general managers also ignored them. Because of the pressures involved in mending the city, they seldom attended social events or meetings at which they could mingle with councillors and build relationships. Quite simply, none of this was a priority, compared to other issues we faced. The Council quickly became politicised.

The very nature of our roles requires the council's Chief Executive, Tony Marryatt, and I to work closely together. A minority on the Council appeared incapable of understanding this. We had created enemies when we changed ground rules about developing land surrounding Christchurch. A campaign to get rid of Tony and I has raged ever since.

Tony's employment contract was due to be renewed in the middle of 2011. The Council had to decide whether to re-employ him. If we did, he was due for a pay increase: he had not received one for two years. A committee comprising of councillors Sue Wells, Barry Corbett, Helen Broughton, Glenn Livingston, Tim Carter and myself was established to review the Chief Executive's performance and contract. Independent consultants had reviewed Tony's performance remuneration.

The campaign our enemies waged against us had been effective. Tony and I had both been undermined and there was a whispering campaign to get rid of the Chief Executive.

I posed a question at the committee's meetings about whether this was an appropriate time to be considering not renewing Tony's contract. We were in the middle of the biggest disaster faced by any New Zealand council. His team of general managers had performed magnificently during the crisis and, although there was controversy surrounding Tony, I believed his continued involvement was essential for the city's well being.

This was misconstrued as cronyism. It was nothing of the sort. In view of the knowledge and experience Tony had accumulated about the city and its services, I found it inconceivable that anyone would consider replacing him at this stage with another chief executive.

The threat was compounded by the impact his departure could have on other executives. Some had indicated that if their boss walked, they would too.

It was obvious that his staff liked him. He had made improvements to the team, he had provided certainty, he had promoted good people in the right jobs and he had developed a team of competent people. Surveys show that prior to him joining the council in 2007, two out of three staff were considering leaving. Morale had improved considerably during his tenure.

Tony is not a person who wants to front before the public. If he wanted to be that sort of chief executive, I suspect he would have sought a job in the private sector instead of the 30 years he has devoted to local government. As a result, the public did not know who he was.

The last thing you want during an emergency is to lose your chief executive. If we lost him, and our general managers, it would take months, probably much longer, to rebuild the knowledge and experience they had accumulated. Given the circumstances, we did not have the luxury of that time available for rebuilding an executive team.

If we dumped him, we would upset our 2500 staff who were already toiling under unprecedented pressures. Many had lost homes. Others lived in damaged houses and faced stresses similar to those confronting everyone else in Christchurch. They worked long hours and performed at levels beyond the norm.

Staff had come to me and said: "Look, Bob, if Tony goes, I don't think I'll stay. He's a great boss. I like working with him.

"My wife doesn't want to live in Christchurch, any more, she wants to go the Gold Coast. We want to get the kids out of the schools here. We don't want to live in the earthquake place, and all the rest of it."

Others expressed concern about what was happening among councillors in regard to Tony. They felt that without Mr Marryatt they would be vulnerable. Therefore, if he left, they too would seek other jobs.

The prospect of breaking up such a vital team would be daunting even in the best times. The predicament in which Christchurch found itself made the prospect irresponsible. Given our circumstances, even if Tony's performance had been only mediocre, and I did not believe it had, dismissing him would have been inappropriate. A wiser approach, if he was not performing, would be to build support systems around him. I did not believe this was necessary.

A vigorous, often terse, debate took place in the confines of the committee room.

I was scheduled to enter hospital after the meeting for an operation on my spine. I was in considerable pain, and exhausted. Before I left, I said that because of the impact the decision could have on the Council if Tony's contract was not renewed, I would have to consider whether I would continue as Mayor.

My objective was to emphasise the seriousness of the decision facing us. If they decided against renewing Tony's contract, it would create a situation so detrimental that we would be unable to deliver all the expertise required for the city's recovery. In those circumstances, I would have to review whether I wanted to continue in a Council that could not fulfill its responsibilities.

That was leaked to The Press newspaper. It could have been disclosed only by somebody attending that meeting. The newspaper headline the next morning was: *Mayor Threatens to Resign if CEO Goes.*

I considered the leak an act of treachery. The meeting was confidential. The public was excluded, and the only way the information could have got out was through somebody breaking the trust of the others participating. It was also a break with a long established convention that words uttered during discussions in committee rooms should stay in committee rooms.

It was the first time in my 20 years in local government that this had happened. Established practice is that even when councillors disagree, or lose a vote, they always leave their disputes in the committee room. Councillors are there to act for the benefit of the greater community, rather than serve their own self interest. This is a practice followed in every council throughout the country.

Eventually, I was forced to withdraw from the review because it was alleged that I had displayed bias by supporting Tony. I considered the accusation unreasonable, but I was concerned that if I did not withdraw, the whole decision-making process might be challenged in court.

I did not participate any further and, instead, put all my energy into preparing the central city plan. I had absolutely nothing further to do with the review, and did not even become involved in interviewing potential candidates.

Councillor Aaron Keown was also forced to withdraw for similar reasons. He fought the allegations in court and won.

I was deeply hurt by the nastiness of the process, and saddened to see established conventions of confidentiality shattered. All councils and businesses, even Parliament, rely on confidential spaces in which they can frankly and vigorously discuss issues in a manner that cannot be done in the open.

My view was that we needed to be able to keep Tony because, if we did not, it would have significant negative consequences for the city. Even if some councillors did not like him, it was not an appropriate time to replace him.

Not everybody in Christchurch business circles fails to appreciate the job Tony has performed for the city. Many have congratulated him for his ethics and for confronting some members of the city's establishment.

Part of our problem was that we do not kowtow to Christchurch's inner circle of business people, some of whom, in my view, want to control the city. We adhered to the Christchurch Urban Development Plan and refused to be coerced away from it. After all, the plan is the will of the public, created after consultation with thousands of citizens for the benefit of the city and its people, rather than for a minority. Despite being threatened and bullied, Tony has refused to digress from the plan.

Neither Tony nor I are members of that elite business cartel. Tony is not a Cantabrian and, although I was born here, I have never been part of that clique.

Not surprisingly, councillors' behaviour over the Marryatt affair and other issues taxed public patience. The Press suggested councillors' performance was appalling. It chastised us for not behaving as well as others in the city who had worked hard to rise above difficulties confronting them.

"…on the contrary, some (concillors) have behaved like recalcitrant children in a dysfunctional family. It is time for them to grow up and start to behave like adults," it chastised in an editorial.

It particularly mentioned first-time councillor, Tim Carter, who had told The Press on 23 January 2012 that he wanted Tony Marryatt sacked. He called for the Government to replace him with a Commissioner.

In a statement to The Press, he accused Tony and I of bad leadership.

Cr Carter is the nephew of the Minister of Local Government, David Carter, whose father, Maurice Carter, served on the Council for 36 years. Cr Carter's father, Philip, (David Carter's brother) was also on the Council and is regarded as Christchurch's richest man.

Maurice Carter emigrated from Yorkshire and established a Christchurch property dynasty.

The Carter Group's headquarters was housed in the Regent Theatre building in Cathedral Square. It was extensively damaged and may well be demolished. Two hotels the group owned, the Holiday Inn Avon and Holiday Inn City Centre, were demolished. Large cracks shattered Philip Carter's new $8 million home on Clifton Terrace, and part of it tumbled down the steep cliffs above Sumner Beach.

Maurice Carter was elected to the Council and the Drainage Board at a time of steady growth in Christchurch.

David Carter, who was appointed Minister of Local Government after his predecessor, Nick Smith, resigned in March 2012, quickly distanced himself from his nephew. He gave an assurance they would not discuss anything in the Minister's "work stream."

As a city councillor, Tim Carter, is Mr Marryatt's employer. Yet, he publicly stated through The Press in January 2012 that Marryatt had to go.

The then Minister of Local Government, Nick Smith, publicly called Cr Carter's comments unprofessional in an interview with Newstalk ZB. He urged councillors to stop the infighting.

"Tim is a member of the Council, he's disagreed with a decision about the appointment of a chief executive and he's now trying to go around the back door and get Government to take his view on an internal debate within the Council and I'm not sure that's particularly appropriate," he said.

The Press editorial described Cr Carter's actions as "particularly inept".

"Not only was it not within the power of the Government to do, but it also potentially exposed the council to liability under employment law. As the chief executive's employer, the members of the council are required to behave towards him in good faith and are constrained by other requirements imposed on an employer. Publicly deploring an employee's conduct, especially after he has recently been confirmed in his position and given a pay increase, without following correct procedure scarcely meets those requirements. Carter may still be dissatisfied with the council's decision to re-employ Marryatt, the long and heated debate over which, it must be remembered, Carter lost, but he should keep his mouth shut except in the appropriate forum," it said.

When the media approached me about Cr Carter's statement, I stated that Cr Carter was playing a destructive game. I explained that, as the editorial suggested, as councillors we were, in effect, Mr Marryatt's employer. An employer making such a public statement about an employee could potentially expose Council to a personal grievance being lodged under the appropriate employment legislation.

Such a personal grievance suit, if pursued, could cost ratepayers millions of dollars.

The Council received a letter of personal grievance from Mr Marryatt on 18 April 2012. The Council had to respond immediately and we attempted to settle the issue in the interests of the city.

After many meetings the following statement was agreed:

1. Tony Marryatt confirmed that he is committed to the rebuild of the City and leading the Council organisation,

and

2. The Council reaffirmed its commitment to Tony Marryatt as the CEO of the Christchurch City Council at this critical time.

It went on to say that the Council values and respects Tony Marryatt's role as Chief Executive and recognises and appreciates the work he has put in over this critical time.

This was passed by the Council and the only money paid in settlement to Mr Marryatt was a reimbursement of his legal costs reasonably incurred in pursuing his personal grievance. For its part, Council adopted the new Council Charter which is intended to effect behavioral change and improve the working relationship going forward.

Some weeks earlier and by the narrowest of votes and without my participation in the process, the Council renewed Mr Marryatt's contract for a two-and-a-half year period. It was a slap in the face, because it should have been for five years. His contract will end less than 12 months after the current council's term finishes in October 2013.

Council also subsequently awarded him a $70,000 pay rise, taking his remuneration to around $540,000. The 14 per cent pay increase was made on the basis that he had not had one for two years. First, it was the local body election that caused the Council to postpone an increase, then the earthquake. By the time the Council reviewed it again, the market rate for his job had moved 13 per cent. It was based on a range of comparable salaries paid to public executives with similar experience, skills and responsibilities. For example, the increase brought Tony into the same zone as other senior public servants in the city, including Roger Sutton, Chief Executive of CERA. At the time, Tony was overseeing the administration of an annual budget of $1.4 billion and a staff of around 2500 people. Mr Sutton was overseeing a budget of less than $50 million and a staff of perhaps 200.

The Council's decision on Mr Marryatt's salary provoked a furor.

In the end, Tony, at the urging of the Prime Minister, declined to accept the pay increase.

Apart from Tony Marryatt, the people most hurt by the debacle were the councillors who did not leak information, and who did not openly criticise our employees in public.

Meetings were strained and negative. There was little joy in working for the Council. The atmosphere permeated beyond the council room, it spread through the entire organisation like a virus.

I explained to maverick councillors that they were not destroying my leadership, they were destroying *our* leadership. They needed to understand that the Council collectively, not solely an individual, created leadership. They might think they were harming Mr Marryatt and me, but they were actually undermining the organisation. Staff was demoralized.

In the midst of all the trauma everyone was experiencing, when people were genuinely stressed and upset, a cabal around the council table was dividing the city and undermining the leadership of us all.

Of course, we will have arguments and disagreements, I said. That is what democracy is about.

But once the majority of the Council has made a decision it's done, that is democracy; you move on. You win some, you lose some. If someone is still not happy then let's have it out behind closed doors. But let's give the community genuine leadership. I urged them not to divide the community the way they were. They would not listen.

It became a crisis when Cr Sue Wells became so sick of the unprofessional behaviour that she told me she could take no more and intended resigning from the Council. She had considered her position for sometime, and I could not change her mind. Publicly, she called for the Government to appoint a Commissioner to replace the whole Council.

I rate Cr Wells as an outstanding councillor and a friend. Putting aside her prodigious skills as chair of the Regulatory and Planning Committee, her departure would skew the balance around the Council table dramatically for the worse. I feared her decision could provoke at least one other councilor into tendering her resignation. This would leave me with a Council that would no longer, in my view, be able to function in the best interests of the city.

Fearing the imminent collapse of the Council, I had no choice other than to ring the Prime Minister and brief him.

"John, this is the situation I've got. I feel you should be the first person to hear it," I told him. "On one side I've got all these guys who are undermining everything. Nick Smith (the former Minister of Local Government) has been concerned about that.

"On the other side, I've got good councillors resigning. They've had a gut's full. They are sick of the tension. They are not enjoying their lives. Their own lives are tough enough. They come in to this place and it is just gut-aching stress.

"You may need to contemplate putting Commissioners into this place, because if I lose these councillors, we've lost the Council. It will not be able to function in the best interests of the city and support central government and the needs of the city.

"We need a good relationship. We don't want a battle."

The Prime Minister said he would discuss the issue with the Minister of Local Government, Nick Smith. Within a few hours I received a call from Mr Smith. We agreed we did not want to disband the Council or replace elected representatives with Commissioners. We needed democracy to continue because enough of it had gone; the Government had replaced ECan's elected representatives with Commissioners, and CERA was in place with all its power. Some people worried about Christchurch's diminishing democracy.

He suggested installing a night watchman who could work alongside councillors.

I welcomed his proposal and suggested he add a few extra points into his appointee's job description. For instance, I needed to keep the Chief Executive, and there were issues between councillors and Tony Marryatt that needed to be clarified in a charter. In his contract, Tony had requested the introduction of a charter to establish a code of conduct to which councillors should adhere. Cr Wells agreed not to proceed with her resignation and try this approach. The crisis was averted, but for a few days our Council had teetered on the brink of total collapse.

Nick Smith's solution was to appoint former Nelson Mayor Kerry Marshall as a Crown Observer. His role was to monitor the Council for the Government, to assist Council address its governance issues and to ensure it functioned effectively to support Christchurch's earthquake recovery.

Mr Marshall noted new councillors were immediately faced with reacting to the earthquake and, consequently, had little induction into their roles.

"Behavioral observations highlighted their ignorance of the Local Government Act and conventional council protocols that in themselves are of significant issue," he observed.

He arranged for councillors to be inducted. He then set about obtaining unanimous agreement that councillors would sign a charter committing them to the good governance of the city and the fulfillment of their statutory responsibilities towards the organisation and staff.

Councillors agreed to:

- Promote and support these principles by leadership and example, always acting in such a way as to preserve public confidence in the Council and its approach to decision making.
- Maintain the respect and dignity of the office when dealing with each other, community board members, staff and the community; uphold the law and act in accordance with the public trust placed in the office of the elected member.
- Respect the role of officers and employees and treat them in a way that engenders mutual respect at all times; this includes complying with the Council's good employer obligation on the provision of clear and agreed strategic direction.
- Ensure that the respect and dignity of the office is reflected in dealings with all elected members, management and the public.
- Adopt a 'no surprises' approach when raising matters of interest or concern by following established procedures and policies, as described in the council's 'Code of Conduct and Governance' statement.
- Acknowledge the council's role as a forum in which individual viewpoints are considered and debated and respect is given to the decisions of the Council as representing the views of the collective.
- Abide by and respect protocols and procedures to communicating with staff outlined in the council's Code of Conduct.

Mr Marshall also audited my office and recommended that it employ additional staff to focus on policy advice and internal and external communications.

"Another benefit of increased administrative support would enable a broader level of formal engagement with community and business leaders as well as the government agencies that have been established to rebuild the city. Establishing and maintaining this structure of enhanced networking is a vital component to successfully manage one of the nation's strategically important cities," he said.

"I recommend renewed emphasis be placed on communication internally and externally from the mayor's office on a regular basis. Residents and the business community of Christchurch and Canterbury want to know what is happening, the good and the bad, both at policy and the implementation level."

His term finished on 1 July 2012. Within a week of Mr Marshall's departure, I considered one councillor had already broken the spirit of the charter.

My work during the earthquakes won a Public Relations Institute of New Zealand award for Communicator of the Year. Ironically, despite the honour and my time in television, radio and the theatre, communicating is an area I feel I have not done as well as I wished during my tenure as Mayor. Communications are the council's Achilles' heel.

Although getting messages across to the public should be my stock and trade, I have found it difficult. It can be a fickle business. We are shackled by constraints that do not confine opponents wishing to take a cheap shot, break a confidence, or distort a truth to snatch a quick headline. While utterances of those of us in positions of authority are confined by a picket of facts, dissidents are not restricted by such barriers.

While we labour under weighty topics requiring lengthy explanations to present a correct perspective, our opponents thrive on sensationalism, emotion and one line sound bites.

While council dissidents capture media headlines with ease, council has exhibited an inability to project its message clearly and strategically. To rectify this, Mr Marryatt instigated a review of the Council's Communications early in 2012. News of that exercise, in itself, generated another round of negative publicity.

The report was completed in July 2012. It said council had developed a fortress mentality.

Stung by public criticisms, often generated by leaked material, and a number of internal miscommunications, trust between the elected wing and the administrative organisation had reached a low ebb.

Staff no longer trusted a number of the elected representatives. They had become reluctant to share information with councillors they believed were determined to undermine them.

It was a 'warts and all' report with a number of recommendations that Tony Marryatt publicly pledged to put into place.

My entry into local body politics in 1991 was opportunistic. A friend suggested I apply to be a councillor on the Banks Peninsula District Council when a vacancy occurred due to a resignation caused by ill health. Because of the circumstances, the position was filled by appointment rather than election. At the next local body election, I was elected unopposed to a full three year term, after which I later served two terms as mayor. I allowed my name to go forward on each occasion because I was keen to make a difference, rather than pandering to the status quo. I am still driven by that enthusiasm.

Working for the benefit of Christchurch has been the most satisfying and stimulating time of my life. Occasionally, pursuing that ideal has brought condemnation that has polarized our community. On reflection, I may have avoided controversy had I communicated some issues more effectively.

At times, the media's barbs have been hurtful, particularly when they have been personal and directed towards my wife, Jo. But overall, the job has been extremely rewarding and enjoyable. It is humbling to be trusted by so many people to make a difference to their lives.

I have long been familiar with the sting of the barbed pens of television and theatre critics. It was only while serving on the Banks Peninsula District Council that I felt the pricks of public criticism and learned that citizens could be much more venomous than any critics I had encountered in the media.

The Peninsula is one of New Zealand's most idyllic places. Its ruggedness has been tamed by Maori, French and British settlers who created a potpourri of culture and charm that is unique in New Zealand.

The Mayoralty there offered a pleasant social life. I could have confined my duties to simply attending Council meetings and mixing with genteel folk at quaint garden parties. However, it is not in my nature to do so.

This was particularly so when I discovered the Peninsula's dark secret – it was going to go broke. While the area was a popular holiday haunt for Cantabrians, not enough people lived there to generate sufficient income to pay its bills.

It could barely afford the upkeep on essential services such as fixing potholes on roads and footpaths, let alone contemplate expensive new essential services such as sewers and articulated water.

Having uncovered the area's nasty little secret, two options confronted me: either fix it or leave the Council. If I fled from the Peninsula's predicament, I would have sat back and watched the District Council gradually collapse under the weight of its financial burdens. That had to be its ultimate fate.

There would be no honour in allowing that, only a warped

satisfaction in saying "I told you so". I cannot accept that that is what is expected of you in life. Instead, if you find yourself in a situation where something needs to be fixed, you are duty bound to stand up and fix it.

The only practical solution to the Peninsula's problems that I could see was amalgamation with the Christchurch City Council. The District Council might have postponed its ultimate fate by selling off tracts of land to create subdivisions. To do so would have destroyed the district's unique environment.

I set about achieving amalgamation, even though I knew it would be unpopular in some quarters. People in places like Diamond Harbour, Akaroa, Governors Bay, Lyttelton and other little pockets of civilization treasured their isolation from the big city. Others accepted the merits of joining forces with Christchurch.

Peninsula residents voted 65:35 for dissolution, which meant we would have to amalgamate with the Christchurch City Council. After amalgamation in 2006, I won a by-election to represent the Peninsula on the City Council.

In one year I had won a Mayoral election on the Peninsula, I had won a major poll, which was like an election, I had then won a by-election and, 18 months later, I won the Christchurch Mayoralty. It was an extraordinary period. It was a period in which, for three-and-a-half years, I fought constant battles. It was an incredibly taxing time. It was a rehearsal for what Christchurch was going to throw at me.

The battle for amalgamation was bruising. It stamped the style of my approach to local government. It taught me much about human nature, planning strategies and setting achievable objectives, and it gave me the confidence to talk to people, regardless of their status, as equals.

It taught me not to balk from making tough decisions, even

if they are controversial. This was demonstrated early in the first term of my mayoralty in Christchurch with the "Henderson properties" and the Ellerslie Flower Show. There have been others: a furor over community and pensioner housing, for instance.

Council owned rental houses and flats were in a disgraceful condition. They were rotting. They had curtains that had not been replaced for years and fell to pieces when touched. They had 1960s vintage hot plates with one little element to cook on. The accommodation was absolutely appalling. Council was guilty of housing tenants in sub-standard accommodation.

Council owned housing had another looming crisis.

Our housing system is self sustaining through its rents. It does not make a call on the ratepayers' pockets. Even so, we are able to offer the accommodation at about 50 per cent below the private market.

The council was not putting aside enough money from these rents to replace aging buildings. With significant numbers of dwellings due for replacement from 2017, there were insufficient funds to replace the decrepit housing stock. Something had to be done. We had to fix it. But to do so, would require a rental increase of 24 per cent which was totally unacceptable to council and the community.

Staff presented us with an innovative proposal: Because our rents were so low, any increase imposed on tenants would entitle them to a further Government rental subsidy. It meant that, in essence, the 24 per cent increase was really only an increase of seven per cent. Coming off such a low rental base line, this translated to tenants paying just a few dollars a week extra.

The proposal meant we could protect the city's commitment as a major housing provider for our most vulnerable, as well as upgrading our existing Council accommodation. It seemed like a winning scheme for all involved. Unfortunately, we did not sell the reality that most people were being subsidised. They were not paying the 24 per cent increase, or whatever it was critics claimed.

The media failed to understand the benefits of the proposal. They condemned it by focusing only on the 24 per cent figure. We were portrayed as a heartless and callous council.

Our decision to proceed with the proposal was subsequently challenged in court. The judgment went against council on the basis that we had not consulted sufficiently with tenants prior to instituting this process. The judge did not criticize the rationale or rental proposals.

After winning the Mayoralty in 2007, I found that although the Council virtually had a room full of great plans about improving the central city area, nothing had been done because of fears of creating a controversy.

When the Henderson land came available, I was determined to seize the opportunity to get something positive happening in the central city. For too long we had shrugged our shoulders and filed it in a too hard basket.

If Henderson's sites had been sold on the open market, they would have been turned into tilt slab buildings akin to that which houses Rebel Sports at South City. We decided to intervene and make something happen. We were surprised that instead of earning applause, we earned condemnation. We had not communicated our vision and motives as clearly as we should.

The same thing occurred with the rebuilding of the City Mall in Cashel Street. We were just finishing it when the earthquake struck. Initially, people hated the idea of creating that Mall. When it was done, they loved it.

Life would undoubtedly be a lot easier if I adopted an approach of doing as little as possible to avoid rocking the boat. It is not in my nature to operate that way and I do not believe I am paid to simply hang the Mayoral chain around my neck and do nothing.

People's reaction to us during the earthquakes was enlightening. We ensured they received information directly from us. They did not hear it from a second or third person who might have distorted it, or could have an axe to grind. I was able to communicate directly with people for a number of months.

My opponents had always denigrated me for being a "quiz show host" or a "show pony", as if what you do as a human being somehow shapes your capacity to succeed at something, or your right to have a say.

Communicating directly, during the earthquakes, enabled people to appreciate the person I am. Unfortunately, it is difficult to maintain that momentum in normal circumstances.

Even though I have been endowed with the grandiose title Communicator of the Year, in reality, I feel I did not deserve it because I failed to win some major battles.

Christchurch is my city. I grew up here. I have fond memories of a childhood of freedom and adventure; a time when I could roam the streets, the plains and hills without the slightest concern.

In those days Christchurch was an egalitarian, smoggy, industrialized, working class city. My father was a tradesman and my mother came from a humble working class family. Her father worked at Flemings Flour Mill near Hagley Park.

Christchurch was famous for its bicycles. Everyone seemed to use one. We would take our bicycles on a train from Heathcote to the city to embark upon great adventures, pedaling through the streets while trying not to lose our balance when wheels got caught in tram track ruts. Often, I had a guitar case strapped on my back as I made my way to Manchester Street to receive lessons from a great musician of the day, Nick Nicholson.

I attended the opening of a new supermarket in Edgeware Road recently and recalled that a retail block opposite had, in my youth, housed Hobdays, a shop that sold model aeroplanes. I would cycle to it from the station to buy balsa wood, glue and, if I was lucky, perhaps even a new plane.

Socially, the city was as flat as its streets. Exceptions were the old money families who grew rich from import controls, subsidies and other economic distortions that favoured the few.

The city's centre, Cathedral Square, was the congregation hub for meeting friends and family; it truly was the city's focal point. That is the reason the city will be successful again. It is still a radial city. Its character is designed to draw its people to its heart.

It is so different from other cities. Auckland is a massive sprawl with many centres. It does not have a single strong core that can be identified as the heart of the city. Even Wellington, although it has a lovely heart, actually stretches up valleys and up the coast. Christchurch, however, grows from a central point. That is one of its saving graces.

In my youth, Christchurch was a low-rise city in which the Cathedral's spire was visible from every corner. I used to climb up the Cathedral, hang off the steeple and be really scared because it was so high.

Sometimes we would get six pence pocket money and take a train to Lyttelton. It cost only three pence each way. We would take the train through the tunnel and go to the wharves to play on the capstans.

Good heartedly, we would shout abuse at seamen who yelled at us. Afterwards, we went to a fish shop in London Street to buy a bag of chips for three pence. Having spent our return train fare, we would walk home over the Bridle Path, a steep track constructed in 1850 to connect the Port to Christchurch.

They were good times, but they could not last for ever. Nor could the city. Even prior to the earthquakes, time had taken a toll on old parts of the city that needed rejuvenation. We had big issues: an ageing population, we were losing young people; we were in a desperate situation and needed to initiate solutions to make the city popular again.

We did, and they would have paid off.

Sadly, it has taken a disaster to get the rejuvenation programme under way.

While devastation from the earthquakes has presented opportunities for creating a modern city, sadly, getting anything started has been frustratingly slow. Delays have taxed everyone. The dilemma is that little can be done until all the parties involved in crucial decisions about land – GNS investigations, EQC, insurers, and so on – are confident about safety.

Tough, often unpopular, decisions have to be made. Ratepayers have a right to know reasons for, and implications of, determinations which will impact on them. Hence our desire to ensure we communicate effectively.

This is particularly pertinent with decisions affecting people's homes. We sympathise with people's frustrations while they await the fate of their damaged homes as experts ponder whether they are eligible for the red or green zone. We understand that they anxiously want to get on with their lives.

Our hands are tied until detailed geotechnical work is completed. Without good data, we are unable to confidently permit rebuilding. Insurers demand this.

Insurers, generally, will accept cover on most things on which they can quantify risk. Without confidence in the precise details of seismic landscape and other impacts, insurance companies will not provide cover because of the number of unknown factors.

Only by accumulating reliable, detailed, house-by-house information can we provide properties with clarity about their safety. With the city being the size it is, this is a painstakingly slow process.

Aftershocks have not helped. We had the first big earthquake on 4 September 2010. Shortly before 22 February, Mr Brownlee and I had posed with jackhammers to symbolically start the first trench for laying pipe not for repair, but for replacement. It was meant to portray a new, positive, phase in the process of rebuilding. Suddenly, we were not just back to square one, we were back to minus square ten; the next earthquake was so much bigger and so much more destructive. The earthquake on 13 June 2011 was even bigger than that of 22 February. And then we had another significant earthquake on 23 December 2011.

Each of those events caused additional damage. They also meant ground conditions had to be revisited and assessed. Of course, underlying them are the 11,000 plus other aftershocks that have undermined progress. All these events slow down the process and scare insurance companies about providing cover.

Obtaining insurance while a contractor builds a house is another problem. A home owner's insurance policy applies from when possession of a house is taken. A contractor must obtain temporary insurance when building a home. Unfortunately, contractors have been unable to arrange cover.

The biggest single issue in getting the rebuild underway has been the difficulty in finalizing accurate data. It is massively complex. CERA, GNS, EQC, Tonkin and Taylor and others have diligently toiled to achieve results. Unfortunately, it does take time. People's lives depend upon it.

It has been stressful for everyone. I look at my own parents. Their house was broken in several places. It is cold. The roof is draughty. My mother lost every single piece of crockery. Every time a little earthquake strikes, their house rattles and shakes. At the time of writing they are still awaiting a decision from their insurers on whether their house will be repaired or rebuilt.

They are not wealthy people. They are a hard working, loving, decent couple in their 80s. They do not make a fuss because they think other people are worse off and need more help than they do.

Their attitude can be replicated among the elderly across the city. In many ways, apart from those who lost family and friends, the elderly are people who have lost the most.

Almost everything with which they were familiar has gone. They grew up in Christchurch. They dated and fell in love. The city was part of their romance; so were dance halls and shops. The homes of all their memories have been destroyed.

As if that is not cruel enough, they have arrived at a place in their lives when starting over again is difficult, perhaps impossible. Their lives are filled with uncertainty. They face all this at a time when the world is moving so quickly.

They are told: "Just go online; you can file your information online". Sadly, there are an awful lot of people for whom the Internet is not something with which they are familiar. Even being told to "do it on the phone" can be more a challenge than a solution. Old people are not quite as sharp, and their hearing is not quite as good as it once was. It is very hard for them.

Those are the people in our city that I feel most for, in many ways. I feel for everybody, but I particularly feel for that generation who built so much of this place and who are confronted with such a difficult task at this point in their lives. Sadly, they are not going to see their city rebuilt.

We have never been able to do much for them, and there does not appear to be a lot we can do now. We cannot speed up the insurance companies. We cannot speed up EQC.

We have said to anybody who cannot occupy their house that

they do not have to pay for that part of the property, they need only pay rates on their land. We have tried to give people a break there. Some people think we should give a 100 per cent rebate over the whole property.

For some time, I have called for reform of the country's rates system. I consider the existing rates system to be very inefficient.

The average person goes to work and Government taxes them. They are left with their net income. Then the Council demands they pay their rates, which are simply tax by another name. Because rates are paid out of net income they are actually paying a second tax. If they were a business, they would be able to write their rates off as a legitimate expense.

Ordinary citizens should have the same rights as businesses. They should be able to offset their rates against income so that it comes out of the non-taxable portion, or enable the tax part of it to be claimed.

Then, to add another layer of tax, Government puts a GST on rates. It is not fair and equitable.

People want Government to help them with rates. Government's answer is to tell local government to stop spending on non-essential items. The implication is that councils cannot manage their books. The reality is that central Government demands we do a raft of work that people are forced to pay for in a most inefficient way. The Government could initiate immediate rates relief if it enabled us to off-set rates against earnings. Indeed, if they stopped taxing us a third time through to GST, they could provide an immediate 12.5 per cent saving on rates.

Our experiences in the earthquakes have not only changed our city forever, they have also changed us. We have all learned we can go further as human beings than we either believed we could, or had given ourselves permission to. That is the strength of what has happened to everyone here.

It has changed us in another way as well. People who have experienced the random and unexpected violence of an earthquake no longer take their environment for granted.

We must never allow ourselves, or others, to forget that New Zealand is literally the product of two huge tectonic plates: the Indo-Australian plate to the West, and the Pacific plate to the East. The gigantic collision between these plates is an unstoppable process that unfolds beneath us day and night. Its violence built our country, and it will continue forever to shape where we live and how we build our dwellings to cope with it.

The spectacular Southern Alps and the great central North Island volcanoes evolved from the tremendous forces unleashed as these plates ground against each other. Look around New Zealand and you can see how these processes have shaped, and are still shaping, the islands. Just because we chose to make our homes and build our lives here does not mean the action will stop. We need to come to terms with this, because we cannot fight it. But we can adapt.

Just like the land, I too, along with most Cantabrians, have been scarred by the terrifying seismic events that rocked our city. When travelling outside Christchurch to other parts of New Zealand or other countries, I remain attuned to the possibility that calamitous events could occur in those towns and cities. I now accept that unexpectedly, within the tick of a second, city streets and buildings can become killing zones. I become acutely aware of danger when passing old masonry buildings. I am uncomfortable in crowded theatres and auditoriums. I find meetings and sleeping in high rise buildings slightly unnerving. I ensure I know where to find the nearest fire escape when I sleep in strange rooms. Like most of us who survived the earthquakes, today I am aware of my mortality and how quickly circumstances can change.

At home, Jo and I have a simple routine in our lives that draws on the quake lessons we learned. We know where keys for vehicles and doors are placed. We have torches by our bed, spare batteries for vital electronic devices, an escape path sorted in our head where ever we stay. We also have an emergency survival kit with a wind up radio, water, first aid, spare clothes including wet weather gear, strong shoes, a couple of days of food, a knife, a small gas powered lamp and mini cooker, rope, tarp and an extra blanket. We also keep spare water stored (and regularly refreshed) on the property. We even place our clothing and shoes in position at night so we can grab them in the dark and escape outside if we need to.

You may think we are getting a little carried away but everyone I know in Christchurch now takes these precautions, and so do wise people around the rest of the country. Household emergency procedures do not take much to set up. But why bother? These things only ever happen to someone else, don't they? No, not any more. The precautions we take might, one day, save a life.

My parents' house has the garage beneath it. I encouraged them to park their car in the driveway outside. It is pointless having a car if an earthquake jams the garage doors shut, or traps the vehicle in a partial collapse. A car can be an emergency survival capsule. It has a heater, a radio and is a dry place to sit or even sleep, if necessary; not to mention its ability to help you evacuate or go to the assistance of others if the roads are clear.

The lesson from Christchurch is quite simple: Bad things do not just happen somewhere else on the television news, they are real; they can happen to us all. They did.

That means they can happen to you.

The geological clock will never stop ticking. Preparation is our best defence against seismic events. In that regard, Christchurch is fortunate, even though we learnt the hard way and at great cost to our people.

We are fortunate because we will have a safer future. Our new city will emerge as one of the world's safest. Through stronger and better design, our buildings will attain new, more stringent, standards of awareness and safety. We are abandoning areas where the dangers can no longer be ignored. Liquefaction, cliff collapse, rock roll, shaking violent enough to collapse modern and apparently safe buildings, are factors for which we must plan and confront not only in Christchurch, but all around our country.

Our new building codes are not the only things to rise from the rubble of the seismic events. More importantly, new leaders with new values will also emerge from the earthquakes. The woman who took water to the old lady down the road, while the ground shook under her; the person who climbed into a building to search for the injured; and our own council worker, Joe Pohio, who died trying to save a stranger. Those are the types of heroes and leaders who shone during the earthquake.

While we celebrate leaders like Sir Peter Blake and Sir Edmund Hillary, who are held in our hearts as icons, they are not all that community leadership involves. Leadership is about what we do now, collectively, in our city. We have a city with thousands of leaders now. Ordinary folk who led by example by stepping up and making a difference.

On many occasions we thought we would die. As a result, we gave ourselves permission to do things that we knew needed to be done. We forgot about the material and pondered how we could help people around us.

I think this motivation lies inside all of us. It does not matter whether we are in Christchurch, Kerikeri or Jerusalem. Wherever we might be in the world, when events such as we have experienced occur, something else within each of us takes over and we accomplish things that we would never normally do. We go beyond what we are as human beings and what we thought we could attain.

I first glimpsed this many years ago when I was filming for a travel television programme that was broadcast in America. They took me down a cave behind Charleston, Westport.

We climbed down rope ladders into a cavern deep beneath the earth's crust. Once there, they enticed me to go further into a deeper chamber that they promised was stunningly beautiful.

I dropped down a tube in the limestone, about as narrow as a manhole opening, to a "squeeze", a narrow tunnel that is half full of water. I lay on my belly and crawled along until I freaked out. I thought that if the ground moved because of an earthquake, I would be squashed.

I told a caver I could not go on.

He promised I would be safe and that I was with experienced cavers, but I could choose to abort the adventure. I chose to continue and was rewarded with spectacular sights very few people get to enjoy. We dropped through waterfalls and straddled cracks down which we could not see the bottom.

Returning to the surface wet, cold and exhausted, I froze at the bottom of the rope ladder in the main chamber, and declared I had nothing left in me to climb out of there.

Although I believed I could not do it, the cavers coaxed me one step at a time up that ladder.

At the top, I collapsed onto the ground. I realised I had never previously tested myself physically or mentally to the extent I had in the past few hours. If I had known what I was going to have to overcome, I would have declined the experience. However, pushing myself further than I thought I could ever go, taught me a great personal lesson. I realised that my potential as a human being was greater than I had known or given myself permission to believe.

And that is the way it is with most of us. Unless we have endured an event like an earthquake, we are ignorant about the potential that lies within. The purpose of leadership courses that have people hanging from ropes, scaling cliffs and crawling on their bellies through mud, is to force participants beyond their comfort zone.

In Christchurch, 500,000 people have reached into themselves and accomplished incredible feats. They overcame fear. They discovered generosity. They found love. They became leaders.

They uncovered all these strengths within themselves. Imagine what that means for the future.

Our children are already showing the benefits of this. Their school results are better than those for the rest of New Zealand. These pupils have often been going to two schools that have merged into one – one goes in the morning and the other in the afternoon because of a lack of classrooms due to the number of schools made unsafe by the earthquakes.

They are living in temporary accommodation and homes that are leaking and draughty and still shaking. Academically, they are achieving excellent results generally above the national average. This is a sign of the force that has been unleashed here.

It is exciting to be living in a city in which people have learned that they can accomplish much more than they ever thought. Rather than crushing differences, and limiting individuals, we need to make Christchurch a city in which people are confident they can accomplish more than they ever imagined. It needs to provide them with structures to enable them to do it.

Our people have learned that. It cannot be taken off them. Eventually, it should even influence the way we govern. That is why we are empowering local communities all over the city to design their own areas. We want the people of Lyttelton, the eastern suburbs and other areas to shape their own futures.

It is so easy for bureaucrats like me and others to climb in and tell them what they should have; how they should do it, take over their planning and have road engineers and other experts tell them what to do. Of course we need to work within our collective means, but in partnership and with mutual respect, rather than with mutual disregard.

The earthquakes have opened doors to opportunities that will enable Christchurch and Canterbury to drive New Zealand's economy for the next decade. Prior to the disasters, we accounted for approximately 20 per cent of the nation's GDP and 15 per cent of its workforce. We are a very productive area, punching well above our weight.

The rebuild will inject more than $30 billion into Canterbury. This, in the short to medium term, will bring about levels of growth similar to those of China. Through that, Christchurch will drive the New Zealand economy over the next decade. Most importantly, the 500,000 people in this province today have a richer and deeper understanding about the preciousness and value of life.

We were given a 19th century city; it was destroyed in a moment of intense violence and tragedy. Out of this comes an unparalleled opportunity. The world has moved on from the pressures that faced our forefathers in the 1800's. Population growth, global climate change, environmental awareness, water, energy, these are shaping our world now. We have an utterly unique chance to respond to these challenges. We must not lose it.

We are going to build a 21st century city. It will be much more people friendly, have sustainable buildings, be focused on alternative transport, cycle ways, public transport and green spaces. We will have a wonderful new inner city community.

Christchurch's future is absolutely unlimited, provided we stop saying we're going to rebuild Christchurch. We are not going to simply rebuild Christchurch. If that is what we do, we may as well pack up and go away because before 4 September Christchurch was a city that was dying. Who wants to replicate that?

In order to harvest the opportunities of the future we need to re-imagine Christchurch. We will need to be bold, to think innovatively, to be prepared to let go of our past ways of doing things. If we can collectively do this then our future is assured. The dreams of our forebears, whether they arrived in canoes, sailing ships or aeroplanes, have one thing in common: A desire for a better quality of life, more personal opportunities, and a secure and safe future for our children. Christchurch will deliver these dreams. Already, we are a city that has more jobs than we have employable people.

We are a city that packaged our risk up in the form of insurance, we sold it to the world; we have been doing it for decades, usually it has been money out with nothing coming in. This time, although the price has been high, we have $30 billion heading back into our economy. This will not only build houses, it will create jobs and all the other services required. It will filter down through the city and create a time of unprecedented economic opportunity. At a time when the world faces unparalleled economic difficulties and uncertainties, we have been given a lifeline. We must not waste it.

Today, Christchurch service companies are flat out and looking for staff. Tait Electronics, a global electronics exporter, is short of skilled engineers and other staff. We are short of builders and all sorts of people, both white collar and blue collar.

Building our new city will result in new people coming to Christchurch. They, in turn, will need houses and jobs. They will generate retail activity and stimulate professional services. There will be new communities, new theatres, new restaurants, new clothes shops, new furnishings shops, new hardware shops and new schools.

Christchurch provides an incredible bubble of opportunity. We will rise again. You can count on it.